National Film Board of Canada Collection

HIGHRISE

By Katerina Cizek
Adapted by Kristy Woudstra

The Towers in the World
& the World in the Towers

FIREFLY BOOKS

A FIREFLY BOOK

Published under license from the National Film Board of Canada by
    Firefly Books Ltd. 2019
Book design and adaptation © 2019 Firefly Books Ltd.
Photographs © as listed on page 77
Adapted from the interactive documentary series HIGHRISE:
    Short History of the Highrise (films) © 2013 National Film Board of
        Canada
    Out My Window © 2010 National Film Board of Canada
    Universe Within © 2015 National Film Board of Canada

First printing

Library of Congress Control Number: 2019937752

Library and Archives Canada Cataloguing in Publication
Title: Highrise : the towers in the world & the world in the towers /
    by Katerina Cizek ; adapted by Kristy Woudstra.
Names: Cizek, Katerina, author. | Woudstra, Kristy, 1975- author.
Series: National Film Board of Canada collection.
Description: Series statement: National Film Board of Canada collection
    | Adaptation of the documentary Highrise. | Includes bibliographical
    references and index.
Identifiers: Canadiana 20190097094 | ISBN 9780228102151 (hardcover)
Subjects: LCSH: Cities and towns—Case studies. | LCSH: Skyscrapers—
    History. | LCSH: Skyscrapers—Social aspects.
Classification: LCC HT151 .C59 2019 | DDC 307.76—dc23

Published in the United States by   Published in Canada by
Firefly Books (U.S.) Inc.   Firefly Books Ltd.
P.O. Box 1338, Ellicott Station   50 Staples Avenue, Unit 1
Buffalo, New York 14205   Richmond Hill, Ontario L4B 0A7

Cover and interior design: Hartley Millson
Editor: Julie Takasaki

Printed in Canada

 We acknowledge the financial support
of the Government of Canada.

The NFB is Canada's public producer of award-winning creative
documentaries, auteur animation, interactive stories and participatory
experiences. NFB producers are embedded in communities across the
country, from St. John's to Vancouver, working with talented creators on
innovative and socially relevant projects. The NFB is a leader in gender
equity in film and digital media production, and is working to strengthen
Indigenous-led production, guided by the recommendations of Canada's
Truth and Reconciliation Commission. NFB productions have won over
7,000 awards, including 24 Canadian Screen Awards, 18 Webbys, 12 Oscars
and more than 100 Genies. To access NFB works, visit NFB.ca or download
its apps for mobile devices.

Contents

Introduction

For most of my life, I disliked highrise buildings. As a 5-year-old, I lived in one on the outskirts of Paris. We were among the first and few residents in a brand-new, 12-story highrise. I remember exploring the empty building, with all its echoing sounds and darkness, and finding it very frightening. I also remember dreading visits to my relatives who lived in Prague's South City, a suburb where identical Soviet-style apartments reach as far as the eye can see. The buildings back then were drab, gray, repetitive and set in an eerily empty, maze-like landscape with no energy, character or human touch — concrete everywhere with little sense of humanity or joy.

However, it wasn't until I visited Moscow in the early 2000s that I began to reconsider my own relationship to the urban and the vertical. I was developing a documentary about a Bulgarian-Canadian who lived in Moscow. He arranged the crew's accommodations, and I was surprised to learn his Moscow was not the one from the postcards.

He had booked us into an "apartment-hotel" about two hours by subway from the city center. Out the window I saw block after block of gray concrete towers. But inside the place was teeming with people and languages from all over the world. On the rickety elevator up to our rooms I met migrant construction workers from all across the former Soviet Union. In the open-air market down the street, I could hear Chechen, Uzbek, Korean, Azerbaijani and Cantonese. I celebrated my rowdiest International Women's Day in a packed restaurant at the base of our tower.

It was my first real experience in a globalized suburb. While some of the crew complained that they wished they were staying closer to the downtown action, it dawned on me that I had been introduced to something far more interesting at the end of the subway line.

When I began work on a documentary project in Toronto, I noticed a similar trend. The documentary included a media project about young mothers who had experienced homelessness. When we met women who were homeless or in shelters, they were usually short walking distances from our weekly downtown workshop. But when they got their own rental housing, suddenly they had hour-long commutes from the suburbs to get to the inner city.

It reminded me of Moscow. Of Prague. Of Paris. I began to reexamine my notion of urban geography

and segregation. I also thought about where urban culture and politics reside. I had naïvely believed the suburbs were simply a retreat for the middle class, but the urban peripheries are overflowing with vibrant communities, diverse cultures, humanity — things that may be invisible to a person just passing by.

Then I started work on a project that eventually became *Highrise*, a multiyear, many-media documentary experiment I created at the National Film Board of Canada alongside Senior Producer Gerry Flahive. For me, *Highrise* is a lens into the uncharted territory of the suburban vertical city, challenging our own perceptions of the urban experience. This book was adapted from three of our projects from *Highrise*: *A Short History of the Highrise*, *Out My Window* and *Universe Within*.

A Short History of the Highrise is an interactive documentary that we created for the *New York Times'* Op-Docs. It charts the 2,500-year history of the highrise, but ultimately, this story is less about buildings than it is about people, the places we call home and how we decide who will live where. If you look closely, seemingly ordinary buildings can reveal the values of the society that has created them.

The second half of the book explores highrise living in cities around the world and features stories from our two documentaries *Out My Window* and *Universe Within*. When we created these projects, we didn't want to just look into people's homes; we wanted to work with residents to cocreate their stories from their perspectives. Many of the stories feature highrise dwellers who harness the power of community, music and art, while searching for meaning in their environments. It was amazing to see how people find ways to repurpose the old and crumbling into the useful and even the beautiful. Other stories reveal the hidden digital lives of highrise residents around the world. These stories challenge us to reflect on how technology has rewired our brains and our relationships, and how we can harness technology to bring about change and improve our collective future.

To be human in the 21st century is — more than ever — to be urban. And yet we have little understanding of what that really signifies. Rather than a narrow focus on the downtown core, we must look to the city's vertical peripheries to learn the power of people making homes and neighborhoods within the context of stark economic, social and racial injustices. It is here where we will find the inspiration for change and the humanity amid the concrete.

— **Katerina Cizek**

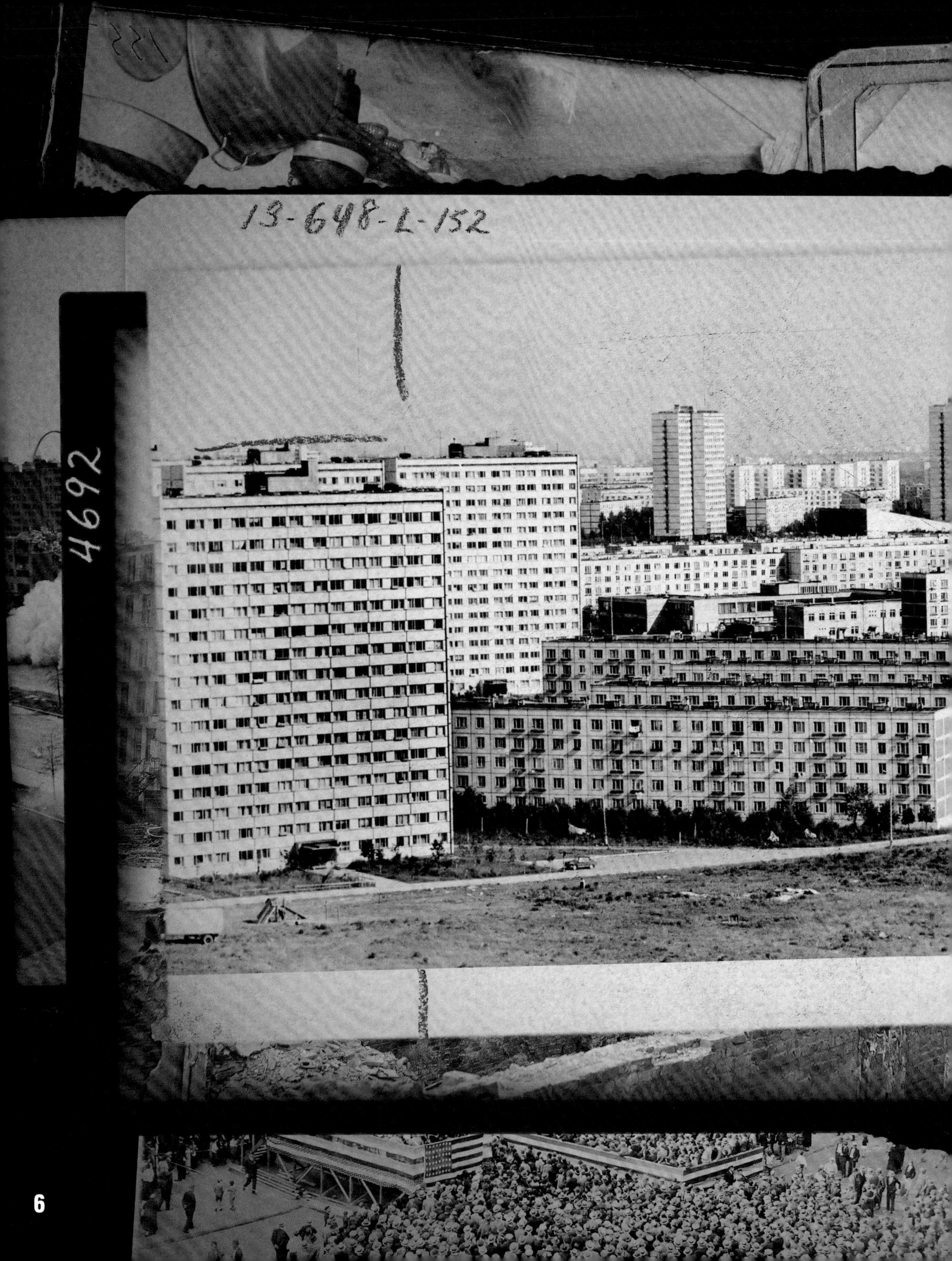
13-648-L-152
4692

A Short History of the Highrise

Some people may look up at highrises and simply see looming structures of brick and concrete and glass. But a closer investigation of where, why and how these buildings were constructed, and who lives in them, reveals so much more. For centuries societies have used the highrise either to house the poor or to protect the rich, and sometimes to reduce the gaps between the two. Through the lens of the highrise, we can see how communities and governments around the world view and deal with inequality and human rights.

Mud
Life in the Earliest Highrises »

It's been a long time we've been placing ourselves in dwellings close to the sky,
And asking ourselves the perennial question: who gets the top floor, and why?

Were these vertical experiments reserved for elites?
Or to warehouse the poor away from the streets?

— A Short History of the Highrise, Mud

Insulae

ANCIENT ROME WAS A BUSTLING metropolis — home to at least a million people by the fourth century. Since the city was surrounded by walls, land was limited and only the very rich could afford a house. The lower classes, on the other hand, had nowhere to go but up.

About 80 percent of Romans lived in apartment blocks of at least five floors. Made of bricks, wood and concrete, these large, square buildings were called *insulae*, which is Latin for "islands." Historians think they got their name because they rose above the ground and had roads and pathways flowing all around like water.

> Many *insulae* had shops such as bakeries or barbers on the main floor, facing the street.

Inside, 40 people could easily live in six to seven apartments. The wealthiest residents (like government employees and businesspeople) were on the more convenient lower floors, with fewer stairs to climb, while the poorest tenants (like artists and teachers) lived at the top.

The cheaper apartments didn't have heat or plumbing and were also less safe. Romans cooked over open flames and used lanterns for light. If a fire broke out, those on the upper floors were the last to get out. As well, the tens of thousands of *insulae* that dominated the city's landscape weren't always constructed very well and would sometimes collapse. (Some landlords were actually happy when this happened because they could charge higher rents once they rebuilt.)

After the Great Fire of Rome destroyed a third of the city in 64 CE, the emperor introduced laws to make the buildings safer. The new regulations included height restrictions, larger spaces between the *insulae*, more access to public water and better-quality building materials.

Insula dell'Ara Coeli in Rome.

236 BCE

Greek mathematician Archimedes invents the first elevator-type device that uses ropes and pulleys to lift heavy objects with little human effort.

191 BCE

Roman historian Livy writes about oxen climbing the steps of a building with multiple floors — the first evidence of highrise construction.

64 CE

The Great Fire of Rome destroys a third of the city. After that, the emperor Nero introduces new laws to make *insulae* safer.

Montezuma Castle

IN THE 1100S THE SINAGUA PEOPLE built a five-story dwelling in the cliffs of northern Arizona. When European settlers found the remains in the 1860s, they named it all wrong. "Montezuma Castle" was neither built by the Aztecs, whose ninth emperor was named Montezuma, nor was it a castle. Archaeologists discovered that the spacious 20-room highrise had actually served as an apartment building rather than a home for royalty.

The "castle" is impressively located 90 feet up a limestone cliff face and likely took several generations to complete. Overlooking Beaver Creek, its position would have protected the families who lived there from attack as well as floods. But getting inside would not have been easy — some historians speculate that residents used portable ladders.

The Sinagua would take clay from the bottom of the creek to hold the limestone walls together and to cover the logs, grass and branches that formed the floors. About 50 people would have lived there at one time. For some reason, possibly because of drought or battles with other groups, they abandoned the building in the early 1400s.

The United States declared it a national monument in 1906. And in 1933 archaeologists discovered other ruins just west of the "castle" that suggest the Sinagua had built an even larger highrise that included about 45 rooms.

In the U.S. and Mexico, Indigenous peoples also built cliff dwellings in the canyons of New Mexico, Utah, Colorado and Chihuahua.

Early Elevators

1 The famous Greek mathematician Archimedes (we can thank him for pi) is also known for his mechanical inventions. Around 236 BCE he came up with a pulley system that lifted large, heavy objects, including ships. This is credited as the earliest form of an elevator.

2 Animal pens and tunnels ran below the arena of the Roman Colosseum, which was completed in 80 CE. Much to the thrill of the crowds, 28 elevator-type devices would lift gladiators and wild animals (such as crocodiles and lions) up to the main stage, where they would fight to the death.

3 In 1743 Louis XV's mistresses could secretly visit his chambers at the Palace of Versailles via a "flying chair" (it actually looked more like a telephone booth). With just a rope, the occupant would lower or lift this "elevator" for one. The king's machinist built the brilliant system, which used pulleys and counterweights.

Montezuma Castle in Arizona.

80 CE

The Colosseum is completed, including lifts that bring wild animals and gladiators up to the main stage.

300 CE

The original Yemeni city of Shibam is built.

315 CE

Rome is made up of nearly 45,000 *insulae*.

1100s

The Sinagua people build a five-story dwelling (now named "Montezuma Castle") on the side of a cliff in the U.S. state of Arizona.

Tulou

IN CHINA'S SOUTHEASTERN province of Fujian, thousands of *tulou*, or "earthen buildings," dot the landscape. Historians believe the Hakka people started constructing these large fortresses for their farming families back in the 1200s as protection from armed thieves.

Often round or rectangular, the *tulou* can reach 60 feet or five stories in height and house as many as 800 people. The thick exterior walls are made of compacted soil, bamboo and stones and are impenetrable to arrows and bullets. Some *tulou* have a granite base that extends deep below the ground, another safety feature in case anyone tried to get in by tunneling underneath.

The Hakka believed in unity and contentment, so the *tulou* did not have a hierarchy. Each family lived vertically, owning a set of identical rooms from the first floor (used for livestock and cooking) all the way to the top floor (their living quarters). Every room was built the same size and with the same materials, windows and doors. Everything else was shared, including bathrooms; water wells; an ancestral hall; and the tea, rice and tobacco fields surrounding the *tulou*.

Each family in the *tulou* owns a vertical set of identical rooms from the bottom floor up.

Tulou in Fujian province.

Some families go back more than 15 generations in the same *tulou*.

In the 1990s young people started to move to the cities in hopes of finding better jobs. Those still living in the *tulou* now make their money from tourism rather than farming. In 2008 the United Nations Educational, Scientific and Cultural Organization (UNESCO) declared 46 *tulou* as World Heritage Sites, calling them "exceptional examples of a building tradition and function exemplifying a particular type of communal living and defensive organization [in a] harmonious relationship with their environment."

1200s

1400s

1532

1743

The Hakka build earthen buildings called *tulou* in China's Fujian province to protect families from attack.

The Sinagua abandon Montezuma Castle.

After a flood devastates Shibam, the city starts rebuilding its mud-brick tower homes.

France's King Louis XV uses a "flying chair" to lift his girlfriend to his quarters at the Palace of Versailles.

Mud Skyscrapers

IN THE 1930S EUROPEAN EXPLORER and travel writer Freya Stark described the Yemeni city of Shibam as the "Manhattan of the desert" because of its mud-brick highrises. However, the walled city was originally built in 300 CE — so maybe New York should have been called the "Shibam of North America."

A devastating flood nearly destroyed the ancient city in 1532, leaving just the mosque and a castle. So Shibam had to rebuild its densely packed tower houses, which can reach 10 stories in height. About 7,000 people, both rich and poor, still live in them today. The city is perched on an elevated rocky area to avoid future flooding and is surrounded by a wall, which was originally built to protect residents from attack.

Masons make the bricks by mixing soil from the surrounding agricultural land with hay and water. Then they leave them out in the sun to bake. To protect the walls and roof from the erosive powers of the sun, rain and wind, they are covered in mud plaster. Then workers add a waterproof layer of lime, which is called *nurah*.

But these beautiful homes still need constant repair. Builders, or

The 2013 edition of *Guinness World Records* listed Shibam as "the oldest skyscraper city in the world."

mu'ellen, have to reapply the mud and lime plasters as they wear away.

Declaring Shibam a World Heritage Site in 1982, UNESCO described the city as "one of the oldest and best examples of urban planning based on the principle of vertical construction," and its architecture as "an outstanding but extremely vulnerable expression of Arab and Muslim traditional culture."

Mud skyscrapers in Shibam.

A Tale of Two Buildings »

By the end of the 1800s, New York City became known for having the world's tallest buildings. However, vertical living looked very different depending on how much money people had. At one end of the scale were the infamous tenements, and at the other was the luxurious Dakota.

The Tenements

The city's population grew exponentially throughout the 1800s as waves of people immigrated from Europe in the hopes of a better life. To accommodate new arrivals, landlords divided up and added onto single-family homes in the Lower East Side of Manhattan. These buildings became known as tenements.

They usually reached five to seven stories in height and were jammed extremely close together on long, narrow lots. The apartments inside were cramped and poorly lit, lacking proper ventilation and plumbing. Because of these conditions, and the lack of indoor plumbing, diseases like cholera spread quickly, killing thousands between 1832 and 1866. By 1900 about two-thirds of the city's population (or 2.3 million people) lived in 80,000 tenements.

Entire families, adults and children, would also work in their homes, which could be the size of half a subway car (325 square feet). Journalist Jacob Riis ›

An illustration from an insurance journal called *The Chronicle* depicting European immigrants landing at Castle Garden, America's first official immigration station.

LANDING IMMIGRANTS AT CASTLE GARDEN.

1814

After the War of 1812, British, Irish and western European immigrants start to make their way to the U.S. by boat, and New York City (NYC) is one of the major destinations.

1840s

Waves of Irish immigrants come to New York, fleeing a horrible famine back home. By 1850 more than 133,000 have settled in the city, and many live in tenements.

1852

Elisha Otis invents the safety brake, stopping passenger elevators from crashing to the ground.

1884

The Dakota, one of the first luxury apartment buildings, is completed in NYC.

LEFT: Photos of tenement residents from Jacob Riis's book *How the Other Half Lives*.

documented life in the tenements in the late 1800s. He wrote about one family that started work at six in the morning, rolling cigars, and didn't finish until nine at night. For every 1,000 cigars, they earned $3.75 (about $103 today). The rent for their two-room apartment was $11.75 ($339) a month.

By the Numbers
How New York City's Tenements Came Down

1867: The Tenement House Act legally defined a tenement for the first time and introduced regulations like requiring one bathroom for every 20 people. But few building owners followed the new rules.

1890: Journalist Jacob Riis published his book *How the Other Half Lives*, which documented tenement conditions in words and photos.

1 in 10 was the infant death rate among tenement residents, which Riis revealed in his book. Readers were shocked and started to demand change.

A ceremony on the Lower East Side of Manhattan in 1933 marks the start of the demolition of the tenements in the area.

2.3 million people lived in New York's tenements by the end of the 19th century.

2 studies of tenements were completed by city officials in the 1890s.

1901: The Tenement House Law came into effect, requiring that units have bathrooms, fire escapes, ventilation and access to light. But some landlords were still slow to make expensive changes to existing buildings.

200,000 new and better apartments were built under city supervision by 1916.

1918: Electricity was required in tenements.

1930S: U.S. President Franklin D. Roosevelt's New Deal (a series of programs designed to help the country recover from the Great Depression) completely changed low-income housing. "Slums" and tenements started to be cleared to make way for public housing projects in the form of highrises.

1890

1892

1900

1901

Jacob Riis publishes his book
How the Other Half Lives
about the living conditions
in tenements.

New York's Ellis Island immigration
station opens. Most immigrants
arriving by boat after crossing the
Atlantic will be processed here.

Two-thirds of NYC's population
is living in tenements.

The Tenement House Law comes
into effect, requiring that all
residents have access to
bathrooms, fire escapes,
ventilation and sunlight.

The Dakota

LIFE FOR RESIDENTS OF THE
Dakota on the Upper West Side
was much different than the
tenements. When the 10-story
highrise was completed in 1884,
multifamily dwellings were still
considered homes for the poor and
working class. But this exclusive
building was geared toward
lawyers, stockbrokers and other
members of the upper-middle class.

No two apartments in the Dakota
were alike. Since elevators weren't
trusted quite yet, the largest and
most luxurious units were on the
first two floors, while laundry and
storage rooms, a gym and servants'
quarters were on the top.

The original 65 apartments
ranged in size from four to
20 rooms. Most had 14-foot
ceilings, wood-paneled dining
rooms and elaborate fireplaces.

The Dakota in New York City.

The grounds included gardens and
tennis courts. If tenants didn't
want to cook, they could eat in the
large dining hall or have meals
sent up via dumbwaiters. Monthly
rents started at $83 and went as
high as $467 (about $2,135 to
$12,015 today).

The Dakota is still one of the
most desirable buildings in New
York, and has been home to many
actors, singers, TV personalities
and company executives. Tragically, musician John Lennon, who
moved into the highrise with Yoko
Ono in 1973, was shot and killed in
the entrance in 1980. ■

People gather near the entrance of the
Dakota hours after John Lennon was shot.

Going Up?
How Elevators Changed Highrise Hierarchy

The cheapest apartments used to be on the top floors of buildings, mostly because of all the stairs tenants had to climb. It took nearly 100 years — and the elevator — to flip people's perspectives.

Hydraulic and steam-powered passenger elevators were around in the early 1800s, but taking one was risky business. They were lifted by ropes, which had the awful tendency to break, causing the elevator car to plummet to the ground — not exactly a confidence booster for passengers.

In 1852 ropes made of wire were introduced to elevator mechanisms. Soon after, Elisha Otis invented the safety brake, which prevented the elevator car from falling if the rope snapped. Despite this game changer, people were still skeptical. A five-story department store in New York City installed an elevator in 1857 because the owner thought the novelty would attract customers. Instead, he removed it three years later when no one was using it.

As the 19th century marched on, technology advanced, buildings got higher and eventually people got used to being hoisted up in elevators. By 1875 office buildings were reaching 11 stories, and working on the top floor soon became a status symbol. The gorgeous views and being away from the dust and noise of the street were too good to pass up.

But when it came to residential buildings, the concept of wanting to live high in the sky didn't come along until the 1920s. That's when architect Emery Roth built two 15-story luxury apartment towers in New York City: the Myron Arms and Jerome Palace. On the top two floors, he included terraces (large balconies) on all four sides, and the penthouse was born.

> In the 1880s, 10 to 20 stories made a building a "skyscraper."

The Myron Arms and Jerome Palace in New York City.

An illustration depicts Elisha Otis demonstrating the safety brake at the 1853 World's Fair in New York City.

Concrete
Highrises Go Social »

> *By mid-century, the state-funded highrise was an iconic emblem of the period,*
> *As one of the most commonly built forms of the century, numerous and myriad.*
>
> *A blunt instrument in the century-long struggle to find a place less obscure,*
> *For those in the middle, somewhere between the rich and the poor.*
>
> — *A Short History of the Highrise*, Concrete

THE 20TH CENTURY WAS THE HEYDAY of the highrise. Thanks to growing urban populations and new technologies like reinforced concrete, steel frames, electricity and elevators, construction of multistory buildings exploded, in both quantity and height, during the 1900s.

Highrises were also no longer meant just for the wealthy (like those who lived in the Dakota) or the poor (like those who lived in the tenements). Governments started building apartment towers to provide affordable public housing for the middle class. "In the 20th century, because of all the wars and ideologies like socialism, it became seen as a big business of the state to intervene in providing a good life for the citizens," explains Miles Glendinning, a professor at Edinburgh University and an expert in mass housing.

Austria's capital city of Vienna completed the first vertical public housing project in 1930. Named after the famous German revolutionary, Karl Marx Hof (or Karl Marx Court) also extends horizontally by more than half a mile and remains the longest residential building in the world. Glendinning describes the seven-story structure ›

In 1909 the city of Helsinki in Finland built the first public housing in the form of four wooden houses divided into tiny apartments for city workers and their families.

Workers in 1947 pour concrete while constructing the James Weldon Johnson Houses, a social housing complex made up of ten 14-story highrises in East Harlem, New York City.

Karl Marx Hof in Vienna, Austria.

Le Corbusier
The Architect of Highrise Life

Artist, painter and pioneer of modernist architecture, Le Corbusier designed buildings in countries all over the world, including India, Japan, France, Iraq, Brazil and the United States. Born in Switzerland, his real name was Charles-Édouard Jeanneret, but in 1920 he took on his pseudonym, which was a variation on his grandfather's last name, Lecorbesier.

He wanted to provide better living conditions in densely populated areas and called his vision the "Radiant City." He thought entire populations should live in "towers in the park" — symmetrical, modern apartment buildings that included stores, restaurants and child care. Green space like gardens, sports fields and cultural facilities would surround the buildings and serve as communal areas.

Steel was expensive during this time, so Le Corbusier designed his buildings to be made mostly from a material that was cheap and strong: concrete. To him, tower blocks were beautiful, peaceful, spacious and affordable. He believed apartments should be assigned to families according to their size, and not how much money they had. "Space and light and order. Those are things that [people] need just as much as they need bread or a place to sleep," said Le Corbusier.

La Cité de la Muette was one of the first housing developments created in the Radiant City style. Completed in the 1930s just outside of Paris, the five 15-story towers were only used as residences for a few years. Soldiers took over when Nazi Germany occupied France during World War II and used them as barracks. Tragically, one building even became a prison camp for Jewish people.

Still, Le Corbusier's ideas continued to influence urban planners for decades. Examples modeled after his "towers in the park" idea include Co-op City, Stuyvesant Town and Penn South towers in New York; Moss Park, Regent Park and St. James Town in

Charles-Édouard Jeanneret, also known as Le Corbusier.

Stuyvesant Town in New York City.

Toronto; Alton Estate in London; and Bijlmermeer in Amsterdam.

Just like many utopian ideals and prototypes, Le Corbusier's didn't always translate well to real life. In fact, many now blame him for failed tower blocks and the downfall of public housing in the 1970s and '80s.

La Cité de la Muette in Drancy, France, was used as a barracks and a prison camp during World War II.

Helsinki, Finland, becomes home to the first public housing project.

The construction of Myron Arms begins in NYC. This is the first residential building to feature a "penthouse" apartment.

Karl Marx Hof — the first vertical public housing project — is completed in Vienna, Austria.

The construction of La Cité de la Muette begins just outside of Paris, France.

The First Houses in New York City.

First Lady Eleanor Roosevelt (center) cuts the ribbon at the formal opening of the First Houses in December 1935.

as "the emblem of the radical spirit."

At the same time, a Swiss-French architect who went by the name Le Corbusier came up with a plan that heavily influenced what mass housing would look like in cities around the world in the years to come. (Read all about him on page 17.)

One of the first public housing projects in the United States was built in New York City under President Franklin D. Roosevelt's New Deal, a series of programs to help the country recover from the Great Depression. Tenements were torn down to make room for the First Houses, a group of eight apartment buildings that opened their doors in 1935. Depending on tenants' income, rent ranged from $5 to $7 (about $72 to $100 today). The need for affordable housing was so great that more

than 3,000 people applied for the 122 apartments.

After World War II, the concept of public housing took off as soldiers returned home looking for jobs and places to live. In Europe many cities needed to rebuild because of extensive bombing. "Households were subdividing, people were having children and getting married," adds Glendinning. "There had been no building in the countries for six

1933

1945

1959

Le Corbusier publishes *The Radiant City*, although he first presented the concept in the 1920s.

World War II ends, veterans return home and a population boom begins, creating a need for mass housing.

NYC planner Robert Moses has built tens of thousands of apartment units in Le Corbusier's "towers in the park" style.

In a residential area of southwestern Moscow, Russia, concrete highrises stretch as far as the eye can see.

years." As a result, highrises and vertical living became symbols of hope for the future.

While every city had its own interpretation of mass housing, there were similarities. The buildings provided modern conveniences such as running water, electricity and indoor toilets. They were often made of concrete and steel and designed in a modernist architectural style — sleek, simple and completely functional.

Putting up residential towers quickly and cheaply even became a point of competition between eastern and western Europe. The goal was "housing for all," and more than 60 million people in the former Soviet Union — from Russia to Kazakhstan — still live in the gray, prefabricated concrete buildings that were constructed during this time.

Words for the apartment buildings made of prefab concrete panels in eastern Europe include *panelák* (Czech), *plattenbau* (German) and *panelház* (Hungarian).

This council housing estate in east London, U.K., was built in the late 1960s in a modernist style typical of the era.

Urban Renewal, Take One

After the Great Depression, New York City's then mayor, Fiorello La Guardia, and his chief city planner, Robert Moses, were intent on "urban renewal." Together they took on controversial development projects that claimed large areas of land, including impoverished neighborhoods, to build highways, beaches, parks, pools and highrises.

Moses continued with this vision long after La Guardia's retirement in 1945. Embracing Le Corbusier's "towers in the park" design, he constructed many concrete highrises surrounded

As part of urban renewal, Moses cleared impoverished areas to make way for new highrise complexes, like this future site of Stuyvesant Town, seen in 1946.

Robert Moses in 1956.

by green space. He didn't drive, but he saw the car as the most important form of transportation, and he divided the city with ribbons of freeways.

"I raise my stein to the builder who can remove ghettos without removing people as I hail the chef who can make omelets without breaking eggs," said Moses in response to his critics.

While many of those towers were public housing, city officials didn't always welcome those who most needed affordable rentals. Between 1953 and 1968, they prevented many people who relied on social assistance from moving into the highrises, screening out single moms, those living with alcoholism and anyone who didn't have regular employment. Instead, the apartments were intended for working families who had never used social assistance.

Moses' tactics have faced much criticism, but no one debates the lasting impression he made on the city. By the time he stepped down as New York's "Master Builder" in 1968, various newspapers reported that Moses had created 13 bridges, over 400 miles of parkways, more than 650 playgrounds and 150,000 housing units in his 44-year career.

The Fall of Public Housing »

In January 1970, burst pipes flooded apartments and electrical systems, cutting power to the rest of the Pruitt-Igoe housing complex.

A Pruitt-Igoe tenant uses her gas stove for heat after the electricity is cut.

BY THE 1970S TOWER BLOCKS HAD generally lost their luster and were no longer symbols of optimism. Instead, they became an emblem of failure. Today, public housing "has fallen out of favor. People are vilifying them," says mass housing expert Professor Miles Glendinning. "They're part of the collective fabric and regarded negatively."

How did we get here? Years of neglect, corruption, lack of funding and poor management caused many buildings to fall into disrepair while neighborhood crime rates soared.

Some public housing units in U.S. cities were so badly built that they had to be knocked down almost as soon as they went up. Pruitt-Igoe, for example, was a large, 33-building complex in St. Louis, Missouri. Designed by architect

Minoru Yamasaki, who would later design the World Trade Center in New York, the project was supposed to set the standard for how to provide better homes for thousands of people living in tenements. Instead, Pruitt-Igoe became an example of public housing plans gone wrong.

Residents started to move into the 11-story buildings in 1954 — and they quickly moved out. The elevators regularly broke down, ventilation was poor, parking was inadequate and gang violence was an issue. The government had also purposefully designed the project to be racially segregated. ›

The first Pruitt-Igoe buildings were demolished in 1972.

1968

1976

1986

An explosion in Ronan Point, a 22-story highrise in London, kills four people.

The final Pruitt-Igoe buildings in St. Louis, Missouri, are demolished, just 20 years after the complex first opened.

Ronan Point is demolished.

By the end of the 1960s, tenants had almost completely abandoned Pruitt-Igoe. And the city demolished all the buildings by 1976.

In London, United Kingdom, a 22-story building called Ronan Point was constructed in the same way as Soviet Union apartments. Massive, prefabricated concrete panels were stacked on top of each other, like a house of cards, which didn't prove to be the most stable. Just two months after opening, a gas explosion on the 18th floor collapsed an entire corner. Tragically, four people were killed and 17 were injured. The damage proved to be irreparable, and the building was taken down in 1986.

New York's public housing projects were dealing with rampant vandalism, drugs and other crimes in the 1970s and '80s. All those highways the city had built as part of "urban renewal" (see page 20) also allowed the mostly white middle class to leave the decaying apartments downtown for houses in the suburbs — they could just drive to work. This caused a further geographic, economic and racial divide.

Safety concerns and derelict conditions started to make people — and governments — in Europe and North America skeptical about public housing.

Partially collapsed Ronan Point in London.

1989

Communism begins to collapse in eastern Europe, also ending the construction of tower blocks.

They often blamed the buildings themselves for the social problems within them. So new construction slowed down and eventually stopped. By the mid-to-late 1980s the only new government-subsidized housing going up on a mass scale was in Asia. ■

Many public housing projects in New York City had volunteer safety patrols.

Five Famous People Who Grew Up in Public Housing

Musician **Mathangi Arulpragasam**, known as MIA, and her family fled Sri Lanka when she was 10 because of the country's civil war. They came as refugees to London, England, where they lived in hostels and council flats (social housing).

Growing up in New York City's projects, **Ursula Burns** never dreamed she would become the first black woman CEO of a Fortune 500 company. "I started [in the Lower East Side]," she said in an interview with *Time*. "And . . . I ended up on the top of some mountains. I have more money, more than my mother would have ever imagined, and I still don't judge my success by that."

"Not having any assured income, we applied for and were assigned an apartment in the new housing project in Plains," reads a plaque on the childhood home of former U.S. president **Jimmy Carter** in Georgia. He continues to be an advocate for affordable housing.

Civil rights activist **Yuri Kochiyama** met her future husband while they were in an internment camp for Japanese-Americans during World War II. After they married, the couple lived in the NYC public housing project called Amsterdam Houses for more than a decade and became close friends with Malcolm X.

Former NHL player **Glen Metropolit** spent a lot of time on the rink in Regent Park, a social housing project in Toronto where he lived as a kid. "I'm so thankful in being able to get out of there," he told the CBC. "It gives me strength. It renews me, even at this age. It gives me an appreciation and reminds me where I came from."

Glass Condo Boom »

On a global scale, it's a dawning of a new millennial age,
Towers made of glass rise, and with them another ideology takes center stage.

Housing is no longer built as a tool for social equity and equilibrium.
It's now a bare financial instrument of market capitalism — they call it the condominium.

— *A Short History of the Highrise,* Glass

WITH PUBLIC HOUSING FALLING OUT OF favor, some North American and European cities saw a complete shift in highrise construction in the 1980s and '90s. Shimmering glass condominiums started to surround and even replace the fortresses of concrete and brick. The goal was no longer providing decent homes for the masses; these buildings were about profit for the few.

Condominiums are made up of individually owned apartments (condos), and their construction is booming all over the world. The Canadian city of

Toronto alone has built nearly 300,000 condo units since the 1980s. While that's great for people who can afford one, their prevalence is contributing to a growing housing gap.

Land is limited in city centers, so developers will sometimes buy up older highrises and turn them into condos. (This tactic doesn't always work, though — read about how tenants saved the birthplace of hip-hop on page 26.) Developers will also tear down buildings with affordable rents to put up fancy towers.

Toronto skyline in 1993.

Toronto skyline in 2017.

1996

The Swedish government starts the Solar Housing Renovation project to improve the Gårdsten social housing project.

1997

Plans to redevelop Dharavi, an informal settlement in Mumbai, India, begin. And Hong Kong starts to build "Concord Block" apartments.

2002

Amsterdam completes its renewal plan for Bijlmermeer, a massive social housing project in the Netherlands.

2008

The birthplace of hip-hop, 1520 Sedgwick Avenue in the Bronx, is sold to developers in NYC.

Some wonder whether these glass condos will even stand the test of time and call them "throwaway buildings." While glass is wonderful for the view, it has its weaknesses as a construction material. Common problems include water leakage and poor energy efficiency. As a result, the towers could require major renovations 15 to 25 years after they're built.

Most governments are no longer building much in the way of affordable housing for people who don't earn enough to buy or rent the sky-high glass units. As well, some landlords are turning apartments into vacation rentals (think Airbnb) to make more profit, which reduces the supply of available housing and drives up prices.

Facing an affordable housing crisis, people with middle-to-lower incomes often have only two options: move to the outskirts of the city, where apartments are cheaper, or rent smaller and smaller units downtown.

Developers have started constructing "micro apartments," which are about the size of a hotel ›

Urban Renewal, Take Two

Remember when New York City cleared out low-income areas to make room for roads and modern buildings? They called this "urban renewal," and the same thing is happening in other cities around the world, including Nairobi, Kenya; Mumbai, India; and Istanbul, Turkey.

Dharavi is an expansive informal settlement in Mumbai, covering more than 400 acres, and is home to as many as a million people. It also sits on valuable land close to the city's financial district.

Eyeing potential profit, international private developers want to tear down the existing homes and shops and build residences, golf courses, shopping centers, gardens, schools and hospitals. But the rebuilding has been stalled for more than 20 years, largely due to concerns over what will happen

Skilled potters in Dharavi.

to current residents.

The plans include providing low-income housing, but Dharavi's residents are understandably skeptical. They worry that the apartments they've been promised will be far too small at just 300 square feet. They're also concerned about losing their small businesses and wonder how they'll make a living once they move into a highrise.

Parts of the movie *Slumdog Millionaire* were filmed in Dharavi.

How Tenants Saved Hip-Hop's Birthplace

The Burj Khalifa Tower, the world's tallest building, is completed in Dubai, United Arab Emirates. It reaches 2,723 feet.

Back in the summer of 1973, a young musician helped invent hip-hop at 1520 Sedgwick Avenue, a 102-unit apartment building in New York City. Clive Campbell, also known as DJ Kool Herc, would hold parties in the building's community room, trying out a new style of music. Using two turntables, a mixer and two copies of the same record, he would have a friend rap while he played grooves during the song.

The exterior of 1520 Sedgwick Avenue in the Bronx, New York City.

DJ Kool Herc, along with other residents and housing activists, fought to keep their homes affordable.

Despite this legacy — and an official designation as the birthplace of hip-hop — 1520 Sedgwick was nearly lost. The building had been in a state-run rent-protection program, which kept its apartments affordable. But the owners wanted to take the highrise out of the program and sell it to the highest bidder. And that's exactly what they did in 2008.

The new owners thought that if they turned the apartments into condos, middle-class homeowners would pay market rates and move to the lower-income neighborhood. But then the American economy plummeted and their plan failed.

In the meantime the rents the tenants paid weren't enough to cover the millions the new owners had borrowed to buy the property, and there was no money for, or much interest in, maintaining the building. Cracks in walls went unfixed, toilets flooded living rooms, and that community room where DJ Kool Herc created hip-hop became a storage area for broken-down appliances.

But Herc banded together with politicians, housing activists and the tenants, holding rallies and press conferences to save and restore 1520 Sedgwick. In 2011 Workforce Housing Group, an organization that secures and preserves long-term affordable housing, purchased the building, restoring the building and protecting the tenants' lower rents and their community.

This micro apartment near downtown Seattle, Washington, is about the same size as a large parking spot.

room (some are smaller than 250 square feet). This form of tiny living increases density (providing more housing to more people), which can be better for the environment. But critics warn that crowded conditions can cause stress and other mental health issues. And what happens when a tenant wants to have a family?

Facing these housing problems, city planners, architects and developers are looking for new approaches to accommodate the masses in sustainable ways.

In New York City's neighborhood of Harlem, a 100-square-foot apartment (about the size of a small bedroom) rented for $1,250 per month in 2015.

Rethinking Housing »

WITH RISING POPULATIONS AND increasing urbanization, there's no question that vertical living is the way of the future. But we have to find ways to make it affordable, livable and sustainable.

Tower Renewal

MANY OF THE CONCRETE RESIDENTIAL highrises from the past century are not aging well. They're largely considered failed social experiments from the modernist era. While some are being torn down, most are just left to decay. However, there is a third option: renewal.

In a nutshell "tower renewal" means transforming, updating and renovating these concrete buildings to make them more sustainable and better integrated with surrounding neighborhoods. A handful of cities have embraced this idea.

"Almost every major European city is surrounded by a periphery of postwar highrises," explains Graeme Stewart, an award-winning architect and tower renewal advocate from Canada. "In my education as an architect, these buildings were really villainized. The buildings were blamed as part of the problem. What I find really exciting about the examples we found in Europe and actually throughout the world [is that] it throws that idea out the window. It's not the buildings, it's actually the system around the buildings. What can you do? How does the neighborhood function?"

Lush gardens, eco-friendly retrofits, accessible retail, better transit infrastructure and vibrant common areas are turning once-neglected highrises into much more livable spaces. "Something as simple as a fruit stand can really begin to transform a neighborhood," says Stewart. "Suddenly you have local access to fresh food, you have a social meeting point, you've created employment."

Here are three examples of successful tower renewal projects found in Europe:

Bijlmermeer, Netherlands

When this massive social housing project of 40,000 units started to go up just outside of Amsterdam in 1966, it was supposed to be a thriving satellite community. However, the grand plans fizzled when jobs and amenities like grocery stores didn't come about, so the buildings began to decline. Thirty years later, in the 1990s, the city decided to invest in the area again, introducing rapid transit and pathways for walking and biking, renovating buildings and creating commercial areas and public spaces. These renewal efforts have been a huge success, making Bijlmermeer a desirable place to live.

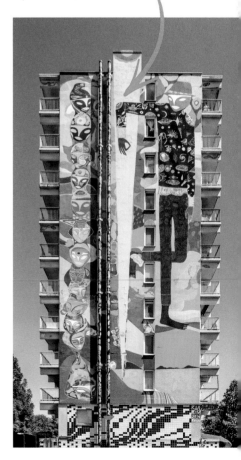

Brazilian artist Rimon Guimaraes painted the side of this apartment building in Bijlmermeer, Netherlands.

2011

1520 Sedgwick Avenue is reinstated as an affordable-living building.

2015

432 Park Avenue, the tallest fully residential building in the world, is built in NYC. At 1,397 feet in height, it boasts 85 floors.

2018

Singapore starts building an innovative public housing highrise that combines housing for the elderly with day-care facilities for children.

Marzahn, Germany

The concrete tower blocks that went up in the 1950s and '60s tend to be leaky, release a lot of greenhouse gases and waste far too much energy. To fix this, some cities, including Berlin, are placing an innovative cladding (a type of covering) on the outside of some of their public housing, such as Marzahn. This environmentally friendly overcladding serves as insulation and stops the leaks. It also improves the livability of the structures (no one likes cold drafts in the winter) and makes them look a lot better too.

Gårdsten, Sweden

Built in 1970 near the city of Göteborg, this social housing project ran into problems from the very beginning. Poor construction caused health problems for its residents, and the buildings weren't well maintained. But in 1996 the government started the Solar Housing Renovation project, restoring apartments, creating beautiful courtyards for residents to gather in and building greenhouses to grow fruits and vegetables. One of the most important aspects of this project is that tenants have been involved in every step of creating a more sustainable and livable community.

Renovated tower blocks in Marzahn, an area of Berlin, Germany.

Solar Housing Renovation in Gårdsten, Sweden.

Going Green
Four Innovations for Sustainable Vertical Living

With climate change and other environmental concerns, some highrises are addressing their impact on the planet by going green.

Gardens

Greenery on rooftops and balconies and in courtyards improves biodiversity, helps clean the air and provides homes and food for wildlife.

Example: Herold Housing Project in Paris, France

Wood and Bamboo

Worried about fires, builders once avoided wood for highrise construction, but now they're embracing its sustainability. Bamboo is also a popular renewable building material because it grows five times as fast as wood.

Example: Sinclair Meadows in South Shields, United Kingdom

Renewable Energy

Buildings get energy from sustainable sources like geothermal and solar panels. Another idea called "passive" housing uses energy-saving tools like heavy-duty insulation, airtight windows and innovative ventilation systems to keep buildings cool in summer and warm in winter.

Example: Pearcedale Parade in Melbourne, Australia

Recyclable Materials

Using recycled or recyclable building materials for highrises reduces waste, energy consumption, carbon dioxide emissions and costs.

Example: Torre Plaça Europa in Barcelona, Spain

Where Public Housing Is Thriving

SINGAPORE AND HONG KONG HAVE continued to build mass public housing long after cities in Europe and North America stopped. With growing populations, waves of immigrants arriving and limited land available for building, the two cities are meeting high demands for affordable housing. And they're doing this in very different ways.

Hong Kong

In the 1980s the city started to build "Harmony Blocks," which are 41-story highrises built in groupings of three. These continued to be the standard for how public housing was built until the late 1990s, when the 40-story "Concord Blocks" were introduced. These buildings had more spacious apartments, with only eight per floor rather than 16.

Tenants share public space that includes parks, playgrounds, gardens, pools and walkways. With such a high population density, shops and other amenities are plentiful and can often be found at the ground levels of the highrises.

The government builds, owns and rents out the apartment blocks. It also offers some tenants the option to buy. Between 1991 and

Shared park space in a Hong Kong housing estate.

Hong Kong, one of the most densely populated places in the world, has a complex public housing system. The seemingly endless number of apartment tower blocks makes for a captivating sight.

Residential Buildings
Century by Century

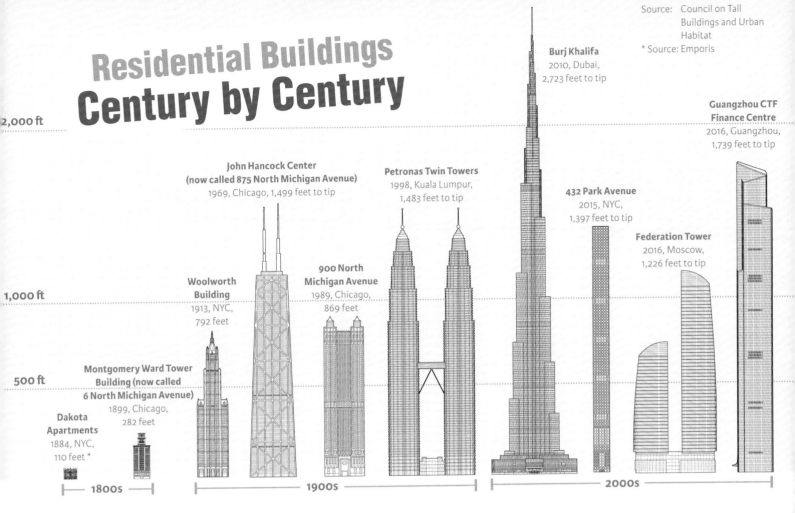

Source: Council on Tall Buildings and Urban Habitat
* Source: Emporis

2,000 ft

Burj Khalifa
2010, Dubai,
2,723 feet to tip

Guangzhou CTF Finance Centre
2016, Guangzhou,
1,739 feet to tip

John Hancock Center
(now called 875 North Michigan Avenue)
1969, Chicago, 1,499 feet to tip

Petronas Twin Towers
1998, Kuala Lumpur,
1,483 feet to tip

432 Park Avenue
2015, NYC,
1,397 feet to tip

Woolworth Building
1913, NYC,
792 feet

900 North Michigan Avenue
1989, Chicago,
869 feet

Federation Tower
2016, Moscow,
1,226 feet to tip

1,000 ft

Montgomery Ward Tower Building (now called 6 North Michigan Avenue)
1899, Chicago,
282 feet

Dakota Apartments
1884, NYC,
110 feet *

500 ft

├─── **1800s** ───┤   ├──────── **1900s** ────────┤   ├──────── **2000s** ────────┤

2001 Hong Kong produced more than 407,000 housing units. Today about 60 percent of the city's population lives in highrises.

Singapore

This city started building mass public housing in the 1940s and had completed 20,000 apartments by 1959. Fast-forward to today, and the government's Housing Development Board (HDB) has built more than a million units. In fact, 80 percent of the population lives in government-built apartments, and the vast majority are owners rather than renters.

Residents have to live in their units for at least five years. This is to avoid "flipping," where people buy a new apartment and sell it quickly for profit.

Unlike Hong Kong's more standardized housing, Singapore seems to thrive on innovation. In 2016 a 47-story building opened called Skyville, which featured communal "sky gardens" and allowed residents to design their layouts. In 2018 a housing development called Kampung Admiralty was being built that combined housing for the elderly with day-care facilities for kids.

It's important to note that, while Singapore has become a model for a thriving public housing system, inequalities do exist. For example, only citizens of Singapore are allowed to purchase new and resale HDB apartments. If you are a noncitizen, you are forced to rent or buy in the increasingly expensive private market. As well, single and divorced citizens (including single parents)

face restrictions for buying and selling HDB apartments that citizens with spouses and families do not. ■

Skyville in Singapore.

The World in the Towers

Amchok's Story
Page 44

Toronto
Page 42

Amsterdam
Page 38

Chicago
Page 58

Zanillya's Story
Page 40

Donna's Story
Page 60

Ivaneti's Story
Page 72

São Paulo
Page 70

Sylva's Story
Page 64

Safa's Story
Page 36

Ling's Story
Page 68

Longxiong's Story
Page 56

Prague
Page 62

Ramallah
Page 34

Guangzhou
Page 66

Tainan
Page 54

Mumbai
Page 46

Nandini's Story
Page 48

John's Story
Page 52

Johannesburg
Page 50

Ramallah

West Bank

Living Under Occupation

Since 1949, Palestine has been made up of two pieces of land that are separated from each other. One, named Gaza, is on the coast of the Mediterranean Sea. The second, much larger region is called the West Bank because it sits on the western bank of the Jordan River. This is where the vibrant city of Ramallah is located.

Most embassies and international nonprofit organizations have their Palestinian head offices here, and the city is the area's hub of culture, politics and finance. While many highrises started to go up during the 1990s and early 2000s, the demand for apartment buildings continues as people move to Ramallah for jobs. Land is very limited, so vertical living is a must.

One way that families create affordable housing in the city is by putting their money together to buy land and construct multifamily dwellings. They do this through the Union of Housing Cooperatives in Palestine. Nearly 60 percent of the cooperatives in the West Bank are in Ramallah. ■

Israel has controlled the West Bank since 1967 in what continues to be the world's longest ongoing military occupation. In 2002 Israel began building a 442-mile wall in and around the region, claiming that it would prevent acts of violence in Israel by Palestinians. According to the United Nations, "the Barrier impedes access to services and resources, disrupts family and social life, undermines livelihoods and compounds the fragmentation of the occupied Palestinian territory."

Along with the wall, hundreds of Israeli checkpoints and other road obstacles limit the movements of Palestinians, who need permits to pass through. Israeli forces can also suddenly close roadways if they believe there is a risk of violence or demonstrations. All of these blockades make it extremely difficult for Palestinians to get to work or visit family members.

Rawabi

A little more than 10 miles north of Ramallah lies a brand-new city built entirely from scratch with private funds, and it hasn't been an easy feat. Rawabi, which is Arabic for "hills" — a fitting choice of name, given the terrain — is the West Bank's first Palestinian planned city.

Designed for the upper and middle classes, Rawabi will have enough highrise apartment buildings, schools, mosques, churches, parks and hospitals for 25,000 people when it's completed. Further construction could expand the population to 40,000. A robust business area means residents can work here too.

However, with Israel controlling land and infrastructure, the city has faced many obstacles and required difficult negotiations. In 2017 Bashar Masri, the businessperson behind the project, told the *Washington Post* that the city could fail if the Israeli military government closes down roads or shuts off the area's water or electricity.

Despite these risks, Rawabi has become a symbol of hope for many Palestinians in a land fraught with violence and tension. "This is a mega project, designed first for Palestinians," Masri told *The Guardian*.

However, some critics have noted that Rawabi is designed first for wealthier Palestinians. The cost of housing in Rawabi is too expensive for most, although on average housing here is more affordable than in Ramallah.

Safa's Story

S AFA LIVES IN THE WEST Bank city of Ramallah in a highrise apartment with her husband, Amer, and their three daughters, Yasmeen, Leena and Zeena. Safa moved here in 1994 from Gaza, which is just an hour's drive away. However, she's only been able to return home to see her parents a handful of times.

Israel requires Palestinians to carry permits to cross through its territory, which lies between Gaza and the West Bank. Because of the political tensions between Gaza and Israel, only certain people, like those seeking lifesaving medical treatment, are even allowed to leave Gaza. As a result, Safa's family

couldn't be present for her wedding or the births of her children. Instead, they rely on technology, such as Skype and email, to stay in touch. But Safa still feels disconnected from her parents, her siblings and the land where she grew up. "Nothing can compensate for a mother's hug, or a father's," she reflects. "Nothing."

Safa's building is nearly empty on weekends because all the young families who live there are out visiting grandparents. This is a tradition she isn't able to carry on with her kids. "I'm one of the people who want nothing more than to wake up one morning and find all the checkpoints gone," she says.

> ## "The children don't have the choices available for a child in Europe, or in America, or Canada."
> — **Safa**

"Ramallah makes you forget sometimes that you're living under occupation, because you don't necessarily see the soldiers every day," says Safa.

Her daughters are still able to take music lessons, go to school and play with friends. But they cannot see extended family, and Safa worries that her girls will not have memories of her parents or her siblings.

"This wall that the Israelis built has closed off some things to us," explains Safa, who would like to see the occupation end. "We've become isolated from other cities, we can't share in the life of family and friends who live outside Ramallah. For me, the occupation is personal. I can't see my family." ▪

Safa's parents Skyping with her from their home in Gaza.

The Digital Barrier

The United Nations believes access to the internet is a human right because of its importance for education, job opportunities, health services and freedom of speech. Concerned that everyone in the world doesn't have equal access to technology, the United Nations has set a goal to "provide universal and affordable access to the internet in least developed countries by 2020."

In 2018 Israel finally lifted a ban on 3G (fast wireless internet service) in the West Bank. (By comparison, Israel has had 3G since 2004 and 4G since 2014.) However, Israel continues to restrict high-speed service in Gaza, citing security concerns. People in Gaza can only make phone calls, and they have very limited access to wireless data.

Fast Facts

Population: 854,047

Area: 85 sq. mi.

Language: Dutch

Amsterdam

The Netherlands

Four Dutch Innovations in Social Housing

KNOWN FOR ITS BIKES AND CANALS, THE capital of the Netherlands also symbolizes the country's rich and long history of social housing. Way back in 1901, the Housing Act declared affordable housing to be a national responsibility. And that legacy continues today.

In fact, the government subsidizes most rentals (75 percent) to make homes more affordable for people with lower incomes. How much do the tenants pay? In 2018 those who earned less than €36,165 (around $41,000) didn't pay more than €710.68 (around $800) per month.

And the subsidized units here don't fit the stereotype of aging, rundown buildings that plagues a lot of public housing projects. Instead, housing associations look after the homes and the whole neighborhood, making sure the area stays clean and safe, maintaining parks and public sports facilities and even getting rid of graffiti.

> The Netherlands was one of the first countries in Europe to pass social housing legislation.

This may seem like a public housing paradise, but some researchers are concerned that the system is in jeopardy. Between 2009 and 2014 new social housing construction was slashed in half in the Netherlands. This was because of budget cuts following the global financial crisis in 2008.

Such a drastic reduction in new builds certainly won't help meet the country's high demand for social housing. Waiting lists are long in many cities — more than 15 years in Amsterdam, for example. So the government is trying to find innovative solutions to fill the gap. ∎

> The Dutch phrase for social housing rentals is *sociale huurwoningen* (so-see-a-le hyur-wone-ing-un).

One size does not fit all when it comes to social housing in the Netherlands. The country's government has found creative ways to help meet the high demand for subsidized homes.

1 **Estate agents for seniors**. When people get older, they often want to live in smaller spaces that are accessible and easier to maintain. One social housing organization in the city of The Hague has an estate agent (similar to a realtor) who helps seniors living in subsidized housing find more suitable, smaller units. This frees up larger spaces for families on the waiting list for housing.

2 **Rent discounts**. Instead of leaving people to suffer on the waiting list, the government offers families in need as much as €300 (around $340) to help subsidize their rent in the private sector.

3 **Energy efficiency**. Six social housing associations are participating in an energy-efficiency pilot project by renovating homes — adding solar panels, better ventilation and airtight windows. The goal is to reduce the energy bills of 111,000 homes to zero.

4 **Abandoned buildings**. Social housing organizations see huge potential in the country's tens of thousands of abandoned buildings. For example, several agencies renovated an empty health-care institute in the southern city of Vlaardingen, turning it into 130 rooms for migrant workers. In the 1980s Amsterdam converted a historic complex of 84 warehouses (called the Entrepotdok) into social housing units.

The Entrepotdok.

"This place is really known for different cultures, and the food, and the vibe, and the ambience."
— Zanillya

Zanillya's Story

MUSICIAN, POET AND actor Zanillya remembers the first time she saw the apartment she shared with her dad. "I was happy, it was summer. I was walking from the subway, and it was only trees and it all looks alike here. It's, like, the same buildings," laughs Zanillya, who was just 15 at the time. "It was like a labyrinth, searching for the place, but it was very beautiful."

She still lives in the same area in southeastern Amsterdam: Bijlmermeer (or Bijlmer, for short), which is now one of the Netherlands' most popular, diverse and vibrant communities. But it wasn't always this way.

Built in 1966, Bijlmer was an ambitious experiment in highrise living. The numerous, practically indistinguishable concrete towers were supposed to be home to 40,000 and employ 60,000, making it western Europe's most completely functional "satellite community." The architects thought they'd created a place where people would aspire to live — even the queen of the Netherlands visited Bijlmer in 1971.

But the plan wasn't fully realized. Roads, transit and other infrastructure weren't properly built, making the area hard to get around. Shopping was also nonexistent. In the end 31 buildings were constructed, containing 13,000 apartment units, but many of them remained empty.

Eventually, those who couldn't afford to live elsewhere in Amsterdam moved to Bijlmer. The housing associations that looked after the area lacked money for maintenance, and the buildings deteriorated. It was not the concrete paradise that planners had hoped for.

In the 1990s, following a tragic

Colorful mixed-use buildings, which incorporate both businesses and residences, have helped revitalize Bijlmer.

Bijlmer ArenA Station.

plane crash into one of the towers, politicians began to reinvest in earnest in Bijlmer. This is also when Zanillya and her dad, Bobby Farrell, moved in.

Bobby, who died in 2010, was a musician, and a pretty famous one at that. In the 1970s he was a member of the disco band Boney M, which had massive hits like "Ma Baker," "Rasputin" and "Daddy Cool." Zanillya says her dad likely chose to live in Bijlmer because the area was quiet and on the outskirts of the city. It's also close to the airport. With all of his travel for concert tours, the location was ideal.

Over the years, Zanillya has witnessed a lot of changes in her neighborhood. The government has renovated buildings, created commercial areas and public spaces, and improved transit. Some of the taller highrises were taken down and replaced by smaller buildings. It's now known for its great diversity. "Like, 138 cultures live in this area," says Zanillya. "[The city] restored it many times, and they are now restoring it, making it more pretty and beautiful every time." ∎

By the Numbers
Dutch Social Housing

4 million people live in
2.4 million social housing units

363 social housing organizations operate the country's subsidized homes

€497 (about $570) is the average monthly rent for social housing

Source: Aedes (Association of Dutch social housing organizations), 2016

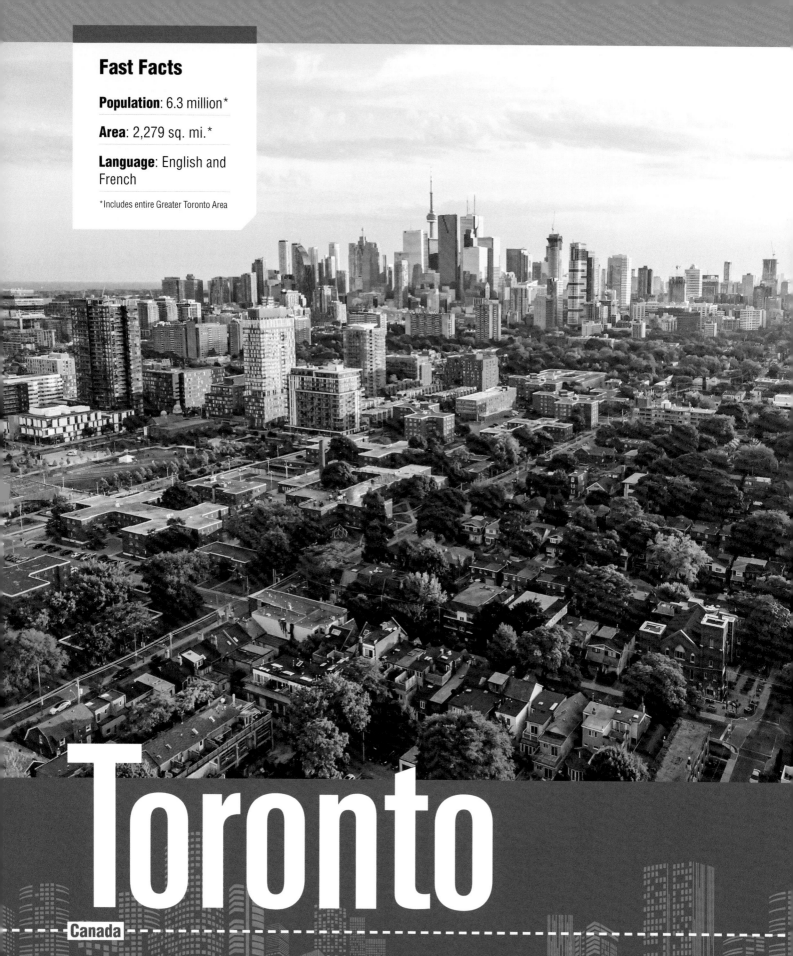

Fast Facts

Population: 6.3 million*

Area: 2,279 sq. mi.*

Language: English and French

*Includes entire Greater Toronto Area

Toronto

Canada

Little Italy, Koreatown, Little Ethiopia — the names of Toronto's distinct neighborhoods reflect the groups of immigrants who settled there to raise families, start up businesses and open restaurants. They also indicate the diversity of the city's population. More than half identify as visible minorities, and 45 percent speak a language other than English or French (Canada's two official languages) at home.

When newcomers arrive in Toronto now, though, they quickly discover that finding a place to live is difficult. Canada's largest city is in the midst of a housing crisis, with vacancy rates hovering around 1 percent. There's an affordability problem too. In December 2018 the average monthly rent for a one-bedroom apartment was CA$2,260 ($1690) — the highest in the country.

Most Toronto renters spend more than 30 percent of their wages on housing — the threshold the Canada Mortgage and Housing Corporation considers unaffordable. And that ratio gets much worse for those who live below the poverty line. Someone earning less than $22,881, for example, could put 90 percent of their income toward rent.

> Toronto ranks second among North American cities for having the most highrises (New York is first).

much in the way of social housing since the early 1990s (applicants can be on waiting lists for longer than 10 years). The city had a surge of concrete towers go up in the 1960s and '70s, but the more recent builds have been soaring glass condominiums, the majority of which are privately owned. More than 290,000 condo units have been constructed in Toronto since the 1980s. Many are purchased as investments and rented out, but the prices can be steep.

Another issue is the rise of online vacation rental platforms like Airbnb. Lured by the possibility of making more money, some landlords have turned their properties into vacation rentals. According to a 2015 University of Ottawa study, Toronto had 4,270 Airbnb listings advertising an entire home or apartment. About half of those were available on the platform year-round, meaning they could have been used for long-term housing. ■

Why aren't there enough places to live? Toronto, along with the rest of Canada, hasn't built

A Vision of Renewal

Award-winning Toronto architect Graeme Stewart sees a lot of opportunity when he looks at the city's concrete apartment buildings that were built in the 1960s and '70s. The majority of these towers are located in the inner suburbs surrounding the downtown core, and they provide 200,000 units in a housing-strapped city. But they need some upgrades.

In his paper "The Suburban Slab: Retrofitting Our Concrete Legacy for a Sustainable Future," Stewart points out that the aging highrises are currently "the most ecologically irresponsible housing type in the city" because they use more energy per square foot than any other type

of housing. The buildings suffer from poor insulation, single-pane windows, electric heating and old mechanical systems. But Stewart doesn't want them torn down. Instead he's a champion for "tower renewal" — making changes to existing structures that will drastically reduce their energy emissions and make them more livable.

Stewart's recommendations include placing overcladding on the outside to create a thermal barrier; adding sun shading to the windows to conserve energy; planting rooftop gardens to help insulate the buildings; and changing the towers' residential-only zoning to allow for

mixed-use spaces, such as shops and day-care facilities. As he told Toronto's city government back in 2007, "This is a housing resource we simply can't lose, and we have to make work."

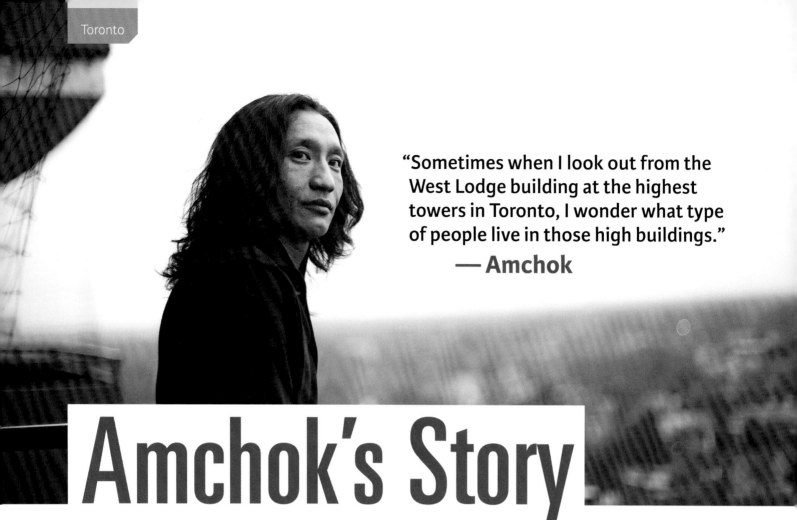

"Sometimes when I look out from the West Lodge building at the highest towers in Toronto, I wonder what type of people live in those high buildings."
— **Amchok**

Amchok's Story

DURING THE WARM summer months, Amchok loves to sit on his 15th-floor balcony overlooking Toronto. He gazes at the passing trains, a nearby church and other buildings below, but his mind often wanders to his first home. So the world-renowned musician will strum his *dranyen* (a Tibetan lute) and play "Pha-yul Gang-jong" ("Homeland the Land of Snow"), a song he wrote as a tribute to Tibet. "When I came to Canada I felt like the weather, temperature and nature of Canadian people are similar to people in my homeland," says Amchok.

He arrived in Toronto in 2006 and found his apartment in a highrise complex called West Lodge, where the rent was cheap. "I think in the past the West Lodge was considered dangerous," says Amchok, who shares his one-bedroom apartment with his wife, Thanglo, and their two sons, Paladin and Jamyang. "Once the Tibetans started moving in, the place has quieted down a bit. . . . These days the reputation has improved."

In fact, his neighborhood of Parkdale has earned the nickname "Little Tibet" because the population is at least 11 percent Tibetan, the highest concentration in the country. It is filled with shops that sell Tibetan goods and restaurants that serve delicious traditional foods, like momos, a type of dumpling. Tibetan monks are often spotted in their long maroon robes.

Amchok's life is very different in Toronto than it was when he was growing up as the son of nomadic herders. "We did not have a good ›

Leaving Tibet

Amchok left Tibet in 2000 when he could no longer play his traditional music. China took control of his homeland in the 1950s, sending government leaders and the Dalai Lama (the spiritual head of Tibetan Buddhism) into exile. Amchok's music, which sometimes praised His Holiness, was considered a form of opposition.

In an interview with the *Toronto Star*, Amchok explained that the Chinese authorities sent a letter to his employer saying he was a troublemaker, bad for the government and shouldn't have a job. He was told he could no longer sing.

"I honor and respect my music . . . and feel that music is like a lamp in a dark room, very precious," he says. Unable to give up his passion, Amchok decided to hike across the Himalayan Mountains to Dharamsala, a city in northern India where many Tibetans live, including the Dalai Lama. There, he was able to perform again.

In 2005 he came to Canada and claimed refugee status, joining more than 6,000 other Tibetans who have settled here, mostly in the Toronto area. "I feel that I have come to a place where I have all the rights and where I can go shoulder to shoulder with every other people in this world."

"Music brought me freedom in life, human rights and a country where I belong."
— Amchok

quality house. It was made out of mud," he says. "I remember that in summertime we lived in tents made out of animal hair. When we looked through the holes, we could see animals all around. . . . Other than that you would not see any motor vehicles, trains or anything you would normally find in the West."

The only highrises he saw were in the movies that came out of Hong Kong. "I used to wonder whether those are in heaven and whether such things could really exist. Now, 20, 30 years later, when I came to Canada, it is such a turn of events in life that I could live in a highrise building." ■

Fast Facts

Population: 18.4 million

Area: 1,681 sq. mi.

Language: Marathi

Mumbai

India

A view over Dharavi.

RANKED AMONG THE WEALTHIEST CITIES IN the world, Mumbai is the financial hub of India. Both of the country's major stock exchanges and all of the banks' head-quarters are located here. It is also home to dozens of billionaires, including the richest person in the country, Mukesh Ambani.

In 2012 the business mogul, his wife and their three children moved into the world's most expensive house — an astounding $1 billion, 27-story highrise. Their home includes nine elevators in the lobby and enough parking for 168 cars. (Despite having a large staff to run such a massive place, the kids were apparently expected to clean their own rooms.)

Just as this densely populated megacity boasts massive wealth, it also has a great deal of poverty. More than 40 percent of the residents live in informal settlements, the largest being Dharavi, which sprawls across 500 acres of central Mumbai. Dharavi is home to over a million people, many of whom work here too.

The area has its own economy, employing residents in such industries as leather goods, embroidery work and pottery. However, developers have been eyeing this land for decades, wanting to turn it into office buildings, entertainment districts and luxury highrises (read more about Dharavi on page 25).

Mukesh Ambani's highrise home, Antilia.

Developers are also profiting from the demolition, reconstruction and sale of residential buildings, which is driving the city's economic boom. Unfortunately, this activity contributes to Mumbai's social disparity by creating homes only the wealthy can afford, while displacing the poor. ∎

On the Move

Shabbir used to travel on the train from his apartment on Mira Road, a massive highrise suburb north of Mumbai, to his job as a stockbroker downtown. Commuting can be a headache in any city, but not many situations compare with Mumbai, which boasts the world's busiest train system.

Every day, more than eight million people use the Mumbai Suburban Railway, and the trains are often jam-packed. The nine-car trains are meant to hold 1,700 passengers, but they often carry over 4,500 during rush hour.

Shabbir remembers one morning when he was late and missed his usual train. He ended up on an overcrowded car, hanging out the doors because there wasn't enough room inside. This is a common way to ride Mumbai's trains, but it's also extremely dangerous. In 2017 more than 3,000 people died on the tracks, many as a result of falling from trains.

"Five minutes, seven minutes on a fast train; it is very difficult to hold on," remembers Shabbir. But he was lucky — a fellow passenger held on to his pants to make sure he didn't fall. After his terrifying ride, Shabbir decided to find a job closer to home, and he now works as a real estate agent, selling highrise units.

To help alleviate the overcrowding and congestion, the city opened the first line of a rapid transit system called the Mumbai Metro in 2014. It is being built in three phases over 15 years and will eventually cover more than 120 miles.

Shabbir's scary commute on an overcrowded train motivated him to find work closer to home.

Nandini's Story

I N MAY 2007 HUNDREDS OF police officers and thousands of city workers pulled up in trucks to the Campa Cola Compound in Worli, a neighborhood in southern Mumbai. They had tear gas and sledgehammers, ready to start tearing down the buildings. "It was very, very, very scary," remembers Nandini, who has lived in Campa Cola for more than 20 years. "We had women, men, kids crying. Some were hysterical."

Built in the 1980s, Campa Cola Compound is a group of seven highrises, ranging between six and 20 stories. Nandini's husband bought a flat on the 10th floor of one building in 1988, and she moved in several years later when they got married. The couple now has two daughters.

What Nandini and other residents didn't realize at the time was that the builders had added more floors to the highrises than were legally allowed. But the city didn't stop construction, nor did it prevent residents from unknowingly buying the illegal apartments. And the city continued to collect property taxes from the residents. Then officials suddenly issued the first eviction notices in 2005. "We are fighting a system which has been ›

In November 2013, on yet another eviction deadline, Campa Cola residents hold the compound's gates to prevent authorities from entering.

"We believe what is happening to us can happen to anybody in India, in any other city. . . . The people who get victimized are the innocent buyers who actually buy [the homes] in good faith."

— Nandini

Deepti and her family were living in their apartment as developers started demolishing her building.

corrupt for years," says Nandini. "And corruption is [from] the grassroots level to the top."

Nandini and nearly 1,000 other residents feared losing their homes. Most were pensioners who couldn't afford to move thanks to Mumbai's sky-rocketing rents. So they organized a "Save Campa Cola" campaign and issued petitions, raised awareness, sent letters and even helped file a Supreme Court case — all in an effort to fight their eviction.

As of 2018 the residents had managed to stay despite many ups and downs. They even inspired a story line in an Indian TV show called *Home*. "It was a question of survival for us, and [it was about] saving our homes," Nandini, who helped organize the campaign, told the website CityLab. "We did what we could do."

Not everyone could hold off the bulldozers, though. Deepti lives with her parents in Mira Road, a highrise suburb north of the city, where 70 percent of the buildings are deemed "illegal." When she was 18, she worked with her neighbors to fight the demolition, but she came home one day to find half the building torn down.

One of India's newspapers, the *Hindu*, reported in 2014 that more than 56,000 buildings in Mumbai were illegal. Of those, 45,000 were ordered to be demolished.

"Paying for the apartment has always been my responsibility. I have sacrificed so much of my child-hood. I've worked alongside my studies," said Deepti at the time. "If that home is gone, then what's the value of all my efforts?"

Stories like Deepti's are why Nandini vows not to give up. "I keep telling everyone, including the kids, that we can put in our 100 percent today, and hope for the best," she reflects. "Whether the [result] is good or bad, you should not look back and say, 'I didn't do my best.'" ■

Johannesburg

South Africa

FROM OCTOBER TO November, Johannesburg's jacaranda trees blanket South Africa's largest city with gorgeous purple flowers. And there's no better place to see them than from the top floors of Ponte City Apartments, Johannesburg's tallest residential tower.

At 54 stories, the highrise is visible from most areas of the city. (The fact that it's round, made of concrete and designed in a brutalist style makes it hard to miss.) This impressive building with its hollow center is so iconic that it has been featured in many movies and even Drake's music video for "Please Forgive Me."

Built in the mid-1970s, Ponte's spacious apartments were meant for white, upper-class residents. The tower oozed luxury, with plans for fancy shops and a ski slope at the base. But as apartheid started to fall and black South Africans and refugees from nearby countries began moving into the downtown core, affluent white residents moved away in what many call the "white flight." They headed for the suburbs, taking their money and influence with them, and the downtown neighborhoods started to deteriorate.

Eventually, Ponte became one of Johannesburg's many "hijacked" highrises. "Hijacking" describes what happens when the owners die or abandon a building, and criminals illegally take over and collect ›

rent from tenants who can't afford to live anywhere else. The city cuts off water, electricity, waste collection and other essential services. Without garbage pickup, Ponte's residents would toss their bags into the tower's immense hollow center. The trash heap is now the stuff of legend — rumored to have reached anywhere between three and 14 stories high. It seemed the higher the garbage piled up, the more Ponte's reputation fell. Soon it became known as a dangerous place to live.

Demand for housing grew once again in the 1990s, and the downtown started to redevelop. In the early 2000s new owners took over Ponte and began renovations. Now the trash heap is gone, the services are back and the tower is safer for families to live in.

The dizzying hollow center of Ponte City Apartments.

The government ramped up its improvements to Johannesburg in preparation for hosting the 2010 FIFA World Cup. Community reclamation projects are also helping to improve the neighborhood of Hillbrow, which surrounds Ponte. (Read more about this on pages 52–53.) But some advocates have pointed out that gentrification is coming at a price. The poorest residents can no longer afford to live downtown and have to move to the townships, where black people were forced to live during apartheid. ■

Apartheid Explained

Nelson Mandela.

Starting in 1948, South Africa's all-white government enforced a legal system of segregation and discrimination called apartheid. This meant that people of different racial groups couldn't live in the same neighborhoods, go to the same schools or use the same businesses. The white minority took over much of the country's land and money. The black majority suffered violence and oppression under this regime and fought against the brutality.

One of the leaders of the movement to end apartheid was Nelson Mandela, and he was arrested many times for his work. In 1964 he was sentenced to life in prison. At his trial he made the following statement: "I have cherished the ideal of a democratic and free society in which all persons live together in harmony and with equal opportunities. It is an ideal which I hope to live for and to achieve. But if needs be, it is an ideal for which I am prepared to die."

In 1973 the United Nations declared apartheid "a crime against humanity." But it didn't end until after Mandela was let out of prison in February 1990. "Our struggle has reached a decisive moment," he declared on the day of his release. "We call on our people to seize this moment so that the process towards democracy is rapid and uninterrupted. We have waited too long for our freedom."

Mandela became president of South Africa in 1994.

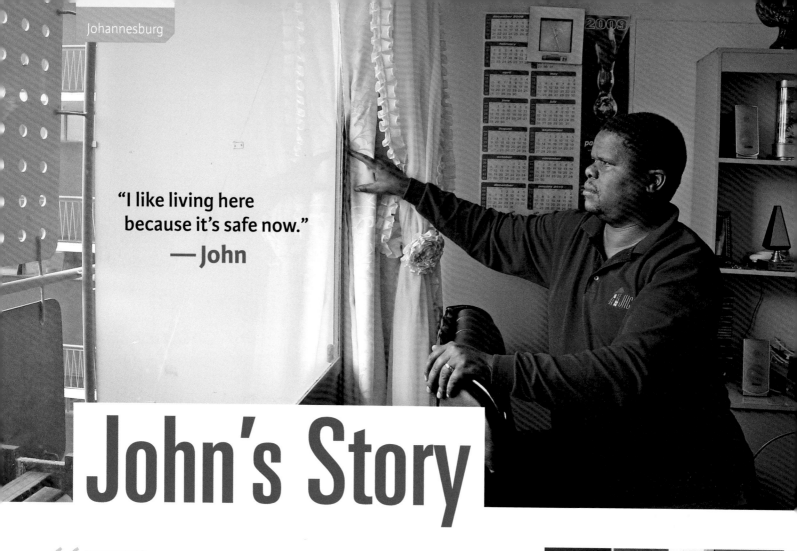

"I like living here because it's safe now."
— John

John's Story

"THE THING I LIKE ABOUT this building is that we work with one another as well as just live here," says John about his highrise. "The units themselves are nice because there is a little balcony that we use for *braais* (BBQ). The view of the city is great from up here."

John has lived in Johannesburg's neighborhood of Hillbrow since 1992. He rents an apartment in a building called Cresthill Mansions, where he also works as a supervisor doing general maintenance and making sure residents don't make too much noise. "The place was already renovated [when I moved in], but I know it was pretty bad before."

Cresthill had been "hijacked," or taken over by criminals, and cut off from any city services until residents and housing advocates joined forces to create the eKhaya Neighbourhood Project. EKhaya, which means "at home" in Zulu, is run by a number of nonprofits, highrise owners, residents and the city. Essentially, they're working together to help make Hillbrow a safe and more positive place to live in.

John volunteers with eKhaya and has won numerous awards for his service — he doesn't even have enough room to display them all. He tries to get as many buildings on board with the community development as possible, which isn't always easy. "Initially, we had

John at work in his office in Cresthill Mansions.

to convince [residents] that we are not here to chase them away but to improve their living conditions," says John.

EKhaya Park in Hillbrow was designed as a safe place for the community to gather and connect.

"What is really positive is that big property companies are starting to invest in buildings in Hillbrow and other big stores are coming here. This means people are now starting to trust Hillbrow. . . . If people are running away it's not good, but when they are coming in it means we have life."

— John

Now the tenants are happier because they have electricity, security guards and better services. Their landlords and building managers are also more accountable. John says crime is down by about 90 percent thanks to eKhaya's security patrolling the streets and alleys and liaising with the police to drive off criminals.

Having a safe community is important to John, especially because of his two young daughters, Queen and Lesego. He would like to see even more improvements, such as expanding a street soccer tournament that he runs a few times a year. "I wish that we could have league matches that we could hold weekly. The tournaments have been key to keeping the community together." ∎

Fast Facts

Population: 1.9 million*

Area: 846 sq. mi.

Language: Taiwanese, Mandarin and English

*Includes both Tainan City and Tainan County, which amalgamated in 2010

Tainan

Taiwan

As one of Taiwan's oldest cities, Tainan has a rich and fascinating history that dates back more than 20,000 years. It was even the capital of Taiwan until Taipei took that role in 1885.

While Tainan's pace of life is more relaxed than that of the capital, it still has a vibrant and bustling downtown with tall buildings, many historical sites and busy shopping areas. However, this isn't where one of the city's more interesting highrises is located.

On the outskirts, overlooking the quiet suburbs, is a towering columbarium, a place for families to store urns containing the ashes of their deceased loved ones. Lung Yen Life Service is a highrise cemetery in a densely populated city where land is limited for both the living and the dead. ■

Most residents here are either Buddhist or Taoist in faith. Tainan has more than 1,600 temples — the most of all Taiwanese cities.

Population Density

Asia includes some of the most densely populated cities in the world. Macau, for example, has more than 50,000 people per square mile and Singapore has more than 20,000. At 1,717 people per square mile, Taiwan may not seem nearly as crowded, until you consider the geography. The island is 13,940 square miles in size, but it's mostly covered by five mountain ranges. This limits where the population of 23.6 million can live. About 90 percent of the people are concentrated along the western coast. So space is extremely precious here.

Highrise Cemeteries

A traditional cemetery in Taiwan.

Lung Yen Life Service in Tainan.

After someone dies, Taiwanese traditionally bury their loved ones underground in tombs that can be on large plots of land — some are as big as a soccer field. But as the population grows on this island, space is lacking and the custom just isn't sustainable.

One solution is highrise cemeteries, like Lung Yen Life Service, the unique multistory columbarium in a suburb of Tainan. Here, families purchase "niches" where they keep the urns containing the ashes of family members who have passed away. The cost of a niche

starts at about NT$40,000 ($1,300) and can easily triple if someone wants to reserve a spot near loved ones. Relatives visit the niches, just as they would a grave in a traditional cemetery, to pay their respects, pray and perform rites, such as burning incense.

Longxiong's Story

"SOME GRAVESITES TAKE up a lot of space," says Longxiong, a resident of Tainan. "I've got one relative, my father-in-law, his tomb takes up almost a soccer field of space. Too big!"

Longxiong believes such large burial sites are wasteful, so he and his family have niches in a highrise columbarium. They can keep their ashes near one another in affordable spaces that, collectively, don't take up too much land.

Longxiong's mother, Huangzhong, regularly visits their family members' urns in the columbarium. When she does, she prays and >

How Much Space Do the Dead Need?

Researchers have done a lot of work to answer that question. According to the calculations of urban planning professors Chris Coutts and Carlton Basmajian, about 76 million Americans will reach the age of 78 — the average life expectancy — between the years 2024 and '42. Burying all those people in traditional plots would take up the same amount of land as the city of Las Vegas (136 square miles).

Wahyu Hariyono of Delft University in the Netherlands predicts that in 2050, nearly 2,500 square miles will be required to bury all the people who die around the world in that year alone. "It is more than five times size of New York City," he writes.

> "In the future, as more and more people die, graveyards are going to overflow. Columbariums, on the other hand, won't let this happen, no matter how many people need space."
>
> — Longxiong

burns incense. She has a lot of relatives here, including her husband, daughter, sisters and parents. The former bookstore owner has reserved niches for her own ashes, and her son's, when the time comes. "I wanted to be near my children, for the convenience of those who come to pay respects," says Huangzhong. "One stop for the whole family." ∎

Three Highrise Cemeteries Around the World

Israel

In Tel Aviv the Yarkon Cemetery was the first to build multistory graves to offset the lack of space to bury the dead. A total of 30 buildings will be constructed in the cemetery.

China

A factory that stands empty in Hong Kong will be turned into an 11-story columbarium for 23,000 urns. The proposed building has been named Le Fabergé because it will resemble the famous bejeweled Russian Easter eggs.

Brazil

The world's tallest highrise cemeteries are 120 and 150 feet high, and they're located side by side in Santos, Brazil. Plans are in the works for an even taller building to join the complex: the 32-story Memorial Necrópole Ecumênica III. Like highrises for the living, the most expensive tombs will be on the highest floors (for the great views of course).

Fast Facts

Population: 2.7 million

Area: 228 sq. mi.

Language: English

Chicago

USA

THE BIRTHPLACE OF THE SKYSCRAPER, Chicago is home to several famous tall buildings, including the super-tall, 110-story Willis Tower (formerly known as the Sears Tower) and the behemoth Merchandise Mart (containing 4.2 million gross square feet, it once had its own zip code). But the city didn't save its ambitious architecture just for business and finance. The American metropolis also applied it to public housing projects in the mid-20th century.

In 1885 the world's first commercial "skyscraper" was complete — Chicago's 10-story Home Insurance Building.

Like so many cities building social housing at the time, Chicago embraced the "towers in the park" (see page 17) design. Tall, concrete residential highrises surrounded by swaths of green space were meant to provide affordable and modern places to live for people who couldn't afford market rates.

One Chicago project was called Cabrini-Green — after St. Frances Xavier Cabrini, an Italian-American nun who was canonized as the patron saint of immigrants, and William Green, a labor leader who advocated for workers' rights. The housing project took two decades to complete.

First, the Chicago Housing Authority (CHA) flattened an impoverished area near the Chicago River to build 586 row houses, which were completed in 1942. Then the CHA constructed 23 highrises in the 1950s and '60s. In total, Cabrini-Green covered 72 acres and housed as many as 20,000 people.

This was all part of then-president Franklin D. Roosevelt's "New Deal," a program meant to kick-start the American economy after the Great Depression. "I see one-third of a nation ill housed, ill clad, ill nourished. But it is not in despair that I paint you that picture. I paint it for you in hope," Roosevelt famously said during his second inaugural speech in 1937. "The test of our progress is not whether we add more to the

Cabrini-Green in 1970.

Cabrini-Green in 2010.

abundance of those who have much; it is whether we provide enough for those who have too little."

Unfortunately for Cabrini-Green and so many other public housing projects across the United States, that test of progress has yet to be passed. Initially, the new units provided much better surroundings than what residents had lived in before, but the haven was short-lived. A complex combination of factors that included underfunding, lack of maintenance and poor management sent Cabrini-Green into decline. The buildings themselves became symbols of the social problems that arose within them, and the city viewed demolition as the solution. ■

"I've been here all my life, so all my memories are going to be gone."
— Donna

Donna's Story

D ONNA LIVED IN Cabrini-Green her entire life, and the buildings held a lot of memories. She laughs when she describes her late grandmother telling her and her sisters to turn down their music, saying they wouldn't have any hearing left. Later, when they were adults and had apartment units of their own, Donna loved being able to run up and down the stairs to visit her siblings. But not all of her memories are good ones.

"As a young girl growing up, I've seen a lot of people die and get killed," she says. "I got shot when I was 13, in my arm. We were jumping rope and the boys just came, and 'pow pow,' start shooting."

Over the years, the media often described Cabrini-Green as "notorious" and "infamous" because of its reputation for gun violence, drugs and gang activity. But what didn't make the headlines were the government's neglect, poor management and lack of funding, which plagued the buildings for decades. In the end public perception prevailed, and many government officials felt the best solution was to tear down the buildings rather than deal with the underlying issues.

In his 2018 book about Cabrini-Green entitled *High-Risers*, author Ben Austen points out that in

"I think if they left my grandma her building, she'd still be alive. But we can't stop what God has taken."
— Donna

the 1990s the U.S. Department of Housing and Urban Development started giving municipalities incentives to do away with large, densely populated public housing highrises like the one Donna and her family lived in. "Nationwide, 250,000 public housing units have been demolished since the 1990s," writes Austen. "Atlanta, Baltimore, Columbus, Memphis, New Orleans, Philadelphia, Tucson — just about

Some Cabrini-Green residents, like Donna and her family, were living among demolition sites for nearly 15 years.

What's Next

Before the last of the Cabrini-Green tenants moved out in 2010, some didn't know where they'd be moving to. They had been told new buildings would replace the old ones, but demolition outpaced construction. As a result, there was a lot of uncertainty.

"You live your whole life in these buildings and then they're gone. You don't know what you're going to do. All your friends are going to be separated and move to different places," said Donna's daughter, Brittany, just before their eviction.

Some Cabrini-Green tenants were given vouchers to help subsidize their rent in privately owned buildings; some became homeless; a select number could live in new mixed-income developments; and many, including Donna and Brittany, moved to other housing projects.

Brittany, who had a hard time with the idea of leaving, commented, "I've got a lot of family [in Cabrini-Green]. I feel safe around my family and the friends I've got. . . . It takes a long time to meet new people."

every American city got in on the action. But no city knocked down as many as Chicago."

In 1995 the Chicago Housing Authority began tearing down the Cabrini-Green highrises. They were to be replaced by smaller, "mixed-income" developments where people from different economic backgrounds could live side by side. Despite residents'

attempts to keep their homes, the wrecking ball started to swing.

"When the crane hits the building, we got to close all our windows because all that dust and stuff, they say it will give us cancer," says Donna, who watched the buildings come down one by one. She and her family lived in the second-to-last tower standing until they were evicted in June 2010.

Later that year, the final tenants moved out of the one remaining highrise, and the building was gone three months later. "I'm going to miss it, but I really won't miss it because we went through something in this community," says Donna pensively. "It needs to be a new community, new things, new environment." ∎

The World in the Towers **61**

Prague

Czech Republic

Central Prague is filled with gorgeous Gothic cathedrals, churches and gateways. But on the outskirts lie buildings of a very different architectural style. That's where the *panelák*, or concrete-block highrises, went up after World War II when the country was ruled by a communist regime.

The idea was to provide a lot of affordable housing quickly and cheaply to help address a shortage of living spaces. So the multistory *panelák* were built with preformed concrete slabs that stacked on top of one another. Clustered together in estates, or *sídliště*, the buildings can stretch more than 300 feet in length and stand 20 stories high. Between 1959 and 1995 more than a million *panelák* apartments were created throughout the Czech Republic.

However, these buildings were drab and gray and weren't considered desirable places to live. After the "Velvet Revolution," when the ruling communist government was toppled, the new leader, Václav Havel, mentioned the *panelák* in one of his first speeches. He called them "undignified rabbit pens, slated for liquidation."

Many thought (and hoped) these symbols of the communist era would be torn down and replaced with more modern buildings. But that didn't happen for a number of reasons, including the sheer

Many *panelák* have had massive refurbishments. Paired with improved infrastructure and attractive landscaping, these buildings are more appealing places to live.

expense. "After the transition from socialism to a capitalist economic system, the state transferred ownership of the apartments under its control, most of which had never been renovated, to municipalities," writes Kimberly Elman Zarecor and Eva Špačková in their 2012 academic paper about *panelák*. "But these cities and towns did not have the resources to manage and rehabilitate the housing stock, so they began to sell the properties to tenants and other buyers."

As ownership transferred, some of the *panelák* were revitalized, including painting the facades in bright colors. The new homeowners could also renovate and increase their units' energy efficiency by improving insulation and windows. However, the success of these changes varied. Some have not been maintained well — or at all. Today about 40 percent of Prague's population lives in *panelák* apartments. ▪

The Velvet Revolution

A series of protests at the end of 1989 in what was then Czechoslovakia brought revolutionary change. Starting on November 17, students gathered in Prague and demanded an end to more than 40 years of one-party rule under the communists. (These demonstrations are also known as the "Gentle Revolution" because the students were peaceful and offered flowers to the riot police who tried to break up their protests.)

Despite the police presence,

the protests didn't end. Instead, they gained momentum — one included an estimated 750,000 people. Eventually, the communist leaders stepped down, and in June of 1990 the country held its first democratic elections since 1946. That's when one of the revolution's leaders, playwright Václav Havel, became president.

Three years later, on January 1, 1993, Czechoslovakia officially split into two countries, becoming Slovakia and the Czech Republic.

Sylva's Story

SYLVA WAS JUST 5 YEARS OLD in 1978 when she and her family first moved into *Jižní Město*, or South City, in the suburbs of Prague. Their apartment was on the top floor of an 11-story concrete building nicknamed "The Great Wall of China" because of its length. "It's a real symbol of South City," says Sylva, who is now a visual artist. "I liked to photograph it because it was morbidly beautiful in its ugliness."

As a little girl, Sylva would play with friends in a nearby muddy valley that had building materials scattered around because the area was still under construction. Back then South City was pretty isolated, without public transit or highway access. There also weren't many amenities in the way of shops or recreation centers. But Sylva didn't notice. "Kids don't see the

A view of South City from above.

world that way," she observes. "Kids don't see the large mass of gray buildings."

South City is home to 200 *panelák*, or prefabricated concrete-panel apartment buildings — the most in all of the Czech Republic. With more than 77,000 people living in an area just over six square miles, it also boasts the

A young Sylva (on the right) with her sister and mother in front of their apartment.

highest population density in Prague.

Sylva still lives here, raising her twins where she grew up. She has seen a lot of change as residents and the government started to revitalize »

The poorly insulated concrete apartment buildings that went up in the middle of the 20th century, including Prague's *panelák* highrises, are big energy wasters. However, simple upgrades can make a huge difference (see A Vision of Renewal on page 43).

Like Father, Like Daughter

"The government is making sure [South City] doesn't turn into a slum. They are investing in renovations, playgrounds and activities for people."

— Sylva

Sylva's dad, Jan, still lives in South City too. He was once a biologist, but now he takes pictures of the area where he raised his family. "I began photographing insects and plants, the things that interest me," he says of his craft. "And I soon found that our built environment began creeping into the frame, even though it's a theme that's ignored."

Within about six years, he had taken tens of thousands of photos of his neighborhood and its concrete buildings. "In the last while, I like to photograph diverse people," says Jan. "People going to work, kids to school. I've also become interested in people who are marginalized."

"Through photography, he became interested in the phenomenon of the apartment neighborhood," says Sylva, who is a photographer as well. "Together, through photography, we became interested in what it means to live here."

South City, painting the buildings in vibrant shades of blue and yellow with red balconies, putting in public transit to the downtown core and retrofitting the highrises so that they are more energy-efficient. "Before, it was a uniform mass, with no little shops. Suddenly, many shops popped up — bakeries, seamstresses," says Sylva.

And remember that muddy valley she once played in? That's now called Central Park and has lush grass with lots of beautiful trees. "Living in an apartment on the periphery has benefits," says Sylva. "We have opportunities to walk in the woods, lots of outdoor sports, which [don't] exist in the [city] center." ■

Guangzhou

China

N AMED GUANGZHOU IN 1921, THIS CITY in southern China actually dates much, much farther back — all the way to 214 BCE, making it more than 2,200 years old. With a population of 13 million, it is now one of the China's largest cities.

As Guangzhou expanded over the years, it grew around the surrounding agricultural land. The city government purchased the farmland but kept the residential villages intact because of the difficulty ›

A narrow street in Xian Village, where demolition and redevelopment has already begun.

The Hukou System

In 1958 China officially enforced the *huji* system, which registered families as either agricultural (rural) or nonagricultural (urban). The system is commonly called *hukou*, which is actually the word for the registration records.

For decades the system was very restrictive, with everything, including where they lived and the social services they received, tied to a family's classification. Those with urban status could access education, pensions and health care, while rural people could own land, but otherwise had to look after themselves.

Over the years the government has made reforms to try to level the playing field. In the 1980s and '90s rural people could move into the cities for jobs (however, they maintained their agricultural status and couldn't use social services). More recently, China legislated a minimum wage and benefits for all workers and allowed children of migrant workers from rural areas to attend urban schools. Still, many inequalities remain.

and expense of relocating the people who lived there. With rentals in high demand, the remaining landowners built up the villages, constructing densely packed multistory apartment buildings with narrow alleys running between them.

These areas are called *chengzhongcun* (villages in the city), and they attract migrant workers from rural parts of China because of their affordable rents. They are vibrant neighborhoods with many shops and food stalls; however, they are often overcrowded and the buildings aren't always well maintained. Nearly 140 *chengzhongcun* lie within Guangzhou's boundaries, and their existence is under threat as the city eyes the land for development.

Since 2008 numerous fancy residential highrises have gone up in Guangzhou to help boost the economy and accommodate the growing population. But land is limited, and some see the village areas as perfect locations for more shimmering glass towers. If new buildings swallow up the villages, though, history will be lost and the current tenants will be left in search of affordable housing, which they likely won't find in the highrises that will soar where their homes once stood. ∎

Ling's Story

EVEN THOUGH LING LIVES in a Guangzhou highrise apartment with her mom and dad, she is keeping a big secret from them. They don't know that Ling is gay. "Compared to other, more open groups in our society, gay and lesbian identity is something very secretive here," explains Ling.

Back in 2007 she was facing a lot of pressure from her family to get married, so she decided to have a "mock marriage," or *xinghun*. This is when a man who is gay and a woman who is a lesbian get married to hide their sexuality because the LGBTQ community still isn't fully accepted in China. Homosexuality was considered a crime until 1997, and was classified as a mental illness for another four years. The stigma persists today. In 2016, for example, the government banned images of same-sex relationships on TV.

Ling found her "husband" on the website QQ, which is the country's equivalent to Facebook. She says people from the LGBTQ community will have a couple of different QQ accounts, one for gay and ›

> "It was only with the rapid increase of internet use in China that mock marriages became possible. We now have this tool of mock marriage, but along with it comes a very misleading or unrealistic way of relating."
> — **Ling**

lesbian contacts and another for those — such as colleagues from work — who don't know about their sexuality.

A month after Ling and her husband met, they got married. But they didn't stay together for longer than a year. "During our marriage, I came to realize more and more of his problems, particularly with his finances," says Ling. "As his partner — which I was, at least from a legal standpoint — I became liable to help support his money problems."

Ling decided it would be better to get divorced. She doesn't plan to try another mock marriage, saying: "I quickly found that this act gets very hard to maintain, and everything became much harder than I had ever imagined. [It's] way out of line with reality." Instead, she is busy as an advocate for LGBTQ rights in Guangzhou. "I think I have come to understand myself much better," says Ling. "I'm ready to take control of my own life and not let societal pressure tell me what to do." ∎

Being LGBTQ in China

In 2016 the United Nations Devel- opment Programme (UNDP) released a report on the largest-ever national survey in China on LGBTQ issues. The extensive results indicate a country in transition.

"The majority of [LGBTQ] people continue to face discrimination in many aspects of their lives, most importantly within the family, where the deepest forms of rejection and abuse reside," wrote Agi Veres, the country director of UNDP China, in the report.

Veres described LGBTQ community members as living "in the shadows," with just 5 percent choosing to disclose their sexual or gender identity at school, at work or in their religious communities. And only 15 percent have come out to close family members.

While many forms of marginalization remain, attitudes are changing. For example, 85 percent of those surveyed support legalizing same-sex marriages in China, and 80 percent believe the rights of sexual minorities should be protected by the law.

Veres wrote that these results are significant developments, but much needs to be done to move toward equality. "Education and evidence-based information, including more realistic portrayals of sexual diversity in the media, have a pivotal role to play going forward."

São Paulo

Brazil

THE RIGHT TO HOUSING IS written directly into Brazil's constitution. However, this South American country is facing a serious housing shortage — millions of people are either homeless or living in inadequate or dangerous environments. One way in which some are fighting for better conditions and safe places to call home is through the organized occupation of abandoned buildings.

In São Paulo, Brazil's largest and richest city, tens of thousands of people have taken over hundreds of empty buildings, including former police headquarters, hospitals, factories and hotels. According to a November 2017 article from *The Guardian*, downtown São Paulo was neglected over the years and became rundown because of poor planning, flooding and rising crime rates. As businesses shut down or moved away, some landowners just

let their buildings remain empty.

Housing advocacy groups map out these abandoned buildings and organize groups of occupiers to move in. The occupiers are diverse and include large families, immigrants, single parents, the elderly and migrant workers.

What they have in common is that they can't afford the astronomically high rents in the city's downtown. They don't want to live on the streets, and they'd like to stay close

Families create functioning households in the abandoned buildings of São Paulo.

to their jobs rather than commute from one of the *favelas* (informal settlements), which are mostly located on the outskirts of São Paulo. There is a shortage of social housing, so moving into abandoned buildings is their best option.

Having been long since forgotten, the structures tend to be in disrepair. So the new residents will move in, clean up and then maintain the premises. Each building (or *cortiço*) has leaders and cleaning schedules, and residents pay a small fee for upkeep. There are also strict rules, such as no alcohol in the hallways or visitors after 11 p.m.

Occupiers never know how long they'll be able to stay. According to Brazil's laws, people can take over any property that no longer serves a purpose, owes taxes or is empty. The police have 48 hours to evict them, but after that the only way owners can empty the place

is through a lengthy and complicated court process. However, evictions do happen, and they can become violent. In September 2014, for example, police used rubber bullets and tear gas when residents occupying the abandoned Hotel Aquarius resisted being kicked out.

Developers and the city government are increasing threats to occupations in São Paulo right now because they want to gentrify or

Protesters take to the streets of São Paulo to defend the occupation movements.

"revitalize" the downtown by tearing down blocks of buildings and replacing them with commercial and mixed-use structures. Given that there is already a huge shortage of affordable housing, this could force even more low-income people out to the fringes of the city. ■

> "I wish that there could be a more sympathetic, dignified, ethical approach to all this exclusion with a view towards combatting it rather than just defending individual political views."
> — Ivaneti

Ivaneti's Story

WHEN IVANETI AND her family moved to São Paulo in the late 1990s, they were in search of work and a better life. Instead, they were forced to live on the streets.

Her husband at the time had lost his job in their rural community. He secured work through a friend in the city, so the couple packed up their kids and made the 250-mile trip to the "enormous concrete jungle," as Ivaneti describes São Paulo.

At his new job, her husband was paid less than minimum wage and it was hard to make ends meet. But when he asked for a raise, he was laid off. Unable to afford rent, they moved from tenement to tenement until their money ran out. "We were overtaken with despair," remembers Ivaneti. "We lived on the streets for three months, almost four, underneath the Glicério viaduct."

Everything changed when her husband met a group of people who invited them to join something called the "Movement," in which low-income people fight for fairer living conditions by moving into one of the city's many abandoned buildings. Skeptical, but tired of not having a roof over their heads, Ivaneti, her husband and their kids joined their first occupation in a hospital that had been empty for nearly two decades.

In this most fitting of settings, Ivaneti says she was "reborn." "I learned about the Movement. I no longer had to see my children starve. Living on the streets, we end up losing our identities," she says. "Without having a place to call our own, we end up falling into an emotional void. It is very hard to find a job, because you're dirty and there is no place to get cleaned up. One has no address, and an address is everything." ›

That was in 1998. Fast-forward to today, and Ivaneti is now a leader of Movimento de Moradia na Luta por Justiça (Housing Movement to Fight for Justice), one of the housing advocacy groups that organizes occupations in São Paulo. "I like the sense of participation. I can no longer just think about the individual; I enjoy cohabitation. I like the joint decisions. It's all about community."

An example of Ivaneti's community showing its strength occurred in 2009. She was standing outside an occupied building with a friend when a woman passed by, pushing her week-old son, Caion José, in a dirty stroller. Ivaneti soon found out that the young mom suffered from drug addiction. "We agreed she and the baby would stay with us and the community would help to care for them," remembers Ivaneti.

Caion José's mom was in and out of the building, sometimes vanishing for weeks at a time. Whenever she returned, Ivaneti would make sure she had a place to eat and sleep. And she encouraged her to feed and play with Caion José, who was now living with Ivaneti. "[She] is not a bad person," says Ivaneti. "She is a victim of crack [cocaine]. She is sick."

Everyone in the occupation would contribute, donating diapers and helping to look after Caion José. "We 'adopted' the baby and his mother," says Ivaneti. Caion José soon earned the nickname "Community." ■

A Symbol of Occupation

Prestes Maia.

São Paulo's Prestes Maia building, a former textile factory, is considered the largest vertical occupation in Latin America. About 2,000 people (nearly 500 families) live in the 22-story building, which has become a symbol of the housing movement in São Paulo.

First occupying the building in 2002, residents worked hard to make it a home, cleaning out garbage and sewage. One woman even had the idea to collect books and open a library. They would host community Christmas parties and Mother's Day celebrations too.

In 2006 the residents worked together to fight off eviction by meeting with the police and staging protests. Rather than kicking the families out into the street, the government finally agreed to provide financial aid to help them find new housing within the downtown area.

The residents gradually moved out and the building was closed in 2007. But Prestes Maia remained empty and abandoned by its owners, so it was occupied again in 2010.

Residents here have a weekly cleaning schedule of communal areas and are expected to abide by rules, including not fighting or making noise late at night. Anyone who breaks the rules has to move to the upper floors, which involves climbing a lot of stairs (the building doesn't have working elevators).

Resources

Links to Highrise

Highrise **home page:** highrise.nfb.ca

A Short History of the Highrise: nytimes.com
/projects/2013/high-rise/index.html

Out My Window: interactive.nfb.ca/#/outmywindow
(needs Adobe Flash Player)

Universe Within: universewithin.nfb.ca/desktop
.html#index (needs Adobe Flash Player)

**Inside *Out My Window* (NFB educational site for
Out My Window)**: interactive.nfb.ca/outmywindow
/educate (needs Adobe Flash Player)

New York Times **Learning Network supplementary
educational material:** learning.blogs.nytimes
.com/2013/10/29/vertical-living-exploring-identity-social
-class-and-global-change-through-the-highrise/?_r=1

Other Links

Global Urban Development: globalurban.org/index.html

The Guardian **Cities:** theguardian.com/cities

Tower Renewal: towerrenewal.com

Tower Block International: towerblock.org

UN Habitat: unhabitat.org

Glossary

Brutalism: A style of architecture characterized by simple geometric forms and the use of raw concrete for construction, popularized in the 1970s.

Capitalism: An economic system in which a country's land and industries are owned and operated for profit by private companies and individuals.

Communism: An economic and political system in which a country's land and industry are publicly owned and controlled by a central government. According to philosopher Karl Marx, the father of communism, the end goal is to create a classless society in which all citizens are economically and socially equal.

Developer: A person or company that buys, develops and sells land and buildings, often to make a profit.

Eviction: Expelling a tenant from a property.

Gentrification: The process of converting a lower-income urban neighborhood into one that appeals to middle- and upper-income people.

The Great Depression: A severe, global economic recession that began in 1929 and lasted throughout the 1930s.

Informal settlement: A residential area to which occupants have no legal claim. The areas are often cut off from basic infrastructure and services, and occupants often live without access to clean water or proper sanitation and in fear of eviction.

Infrastructure: Basic systems and facilities, such as roads, water, sewage, electricity, transportation and so on, needed by a city, country or other area in order to function.

LGBTQ: An initialism for Lesbian, Gay, Bisexual, Transgender and Queer.

Market rate: In real estate, the average price for renting or buying property in a free market. The market rate is determined by a number of factors, including location, supply and demand.

Military occupation: When one state invades and occupies the territory of another state, placing that territory under the authority of the occupier's military.

Mixed-income development: A residential building or area where households from different income levels are blended.

Mixed-use development: A building or area where residential housing is blended with complementary businesses and services, such as office, retail, medical and recreational spaces.

Modernism: A style of architecture characterized by functional, minimal design and the use of materials such as concrete, glass and steel, popularized in the 20th century.

Prefabricated building: A structure assembled using components that were premade in a factory and delivered to a building site.

Public housing: Subsidized housing owned by the government and operated by local agencies. The term is sometimes used interchangeably with social housing.

Social housing: Subsidized housing owned by the government, a nonprofit organization or both. The term is sometimes used interchangeably with public housing.

Socialism: An umbrella term for various economic and political systems in which a country's land and industries are publicly owned and controlled by the government.

Soviet Union: A federation of 15 communist republics in northern Asia and eastern Europe that existed between 1922 and 1991. The Communist Party, based in Moscow, Russia, governed the Soviet Union.

Subsidized housing: Housing for people who require some form of economic assistance from the government or other organizations. Assistance includes public housing, social housing and subsidies for renting market-rate properties.

Vacancy rate: The percentage of unoccupied properties in a particular building or area that are available for sale or rent.

Vacation rental: A residential property temporarily rented to tourists and visitors as an alternative to a hotel. This is also known as a short-term rental.

Acknowledgments

Katerina Cizek

I am eternally grateful for over a decade of collaboration at the NFB with Senior Producer Gerry Flahive and the HIGHRISE dream team: Branden Bratuhin, Heather Frise, Maria Saroja Ponnambalam, Paramita Nath, Kate Vollum, Sarah Arruda, Cass Gardiner, David Oppenheim, Marcus Matyas, Mark Wilson, Elizabeth Klinck, Peter Starr and Executive Producers Anita Lee and Silva Basmajian. We were honored to find brilliant academic partners in Dr. Deborah Cowen, Dr. Emily Paradis, Alexis Mitchell and Brett Story at University of Toronto; and Dr. William Uricchio and Sarah Wolozin at MIT Open Documentary Lab. For our partnership at the *New York Times*, my gratitude extends to Jason Spingarn-Koff, Jeff Roth, Kathleen Lingo, Lindsay Crouse and Jacky Mynt. Heartfelt thanks also to the stellar digital wizards and designers: Helios Lab, Secret Location and Imaginarius. Thanks to architect and tower renewal visionary Graeme Stewart, Elise Hug of the City of Toronto, and the residents and organizers of the Kipling Towers in Toronto — Obi, Pritvanti, Faith, Irene, Maggie, Jamal and Russ — for the inspiration and collaboration. Deep gratitude to my partner in everything, Sean Dixon.

Last but not least, thanks to Steve Cameron and Julie Takasaki at Firefly Books and writer Kristy Woudstra for bringing these stories out of the ephemeral realm of the internet and cinema into the material world of a printed book.

A decade is long; over that time our team worked closely together and, so too, we grieved our losses together. I dedicate this special edition of HIGHRISE to the family who left us too soon: Sarah Flahive, Tamiko Bratuhin, Subrata Ranjan Nath, Neil Smith and Ludmila Cizek. I also dedicate this book to those we welcomed into the world: Isabella Frise, Lipika Dorothea Prins and Ava Dixon. You are the light, the hope.

Kristy Woudstra

Of course, I need to start by thanking director Katerina Cizek for *Highrise*, which has been such an inspiration to me. I was working in international development in 2010 when the NFB released *Out My Window* and I was immediately obsessed by the interactive, heartfelt storytelling. Thank you, Kat, for shedding light on important issues through your unprecedented innovation. Also, I love that I can't pass an apartment building without wondering about all the lives unfolding within its concrete walls.

To Steve Cameron, Firefly's Editorial Director, thank you, thank you, thank you for presenting me with the dream opportunity to adapt *Highrise* into book form. It has been an honor to usher your vision onto the page.

The English language simply doesn't have an adequate word to express my gratitude to my editor, Julie Takasaki. I couldn't have done this without your editorial wizardry and unwavering calmness. Thank you for carrying me across the finish line. Working with you was an absolute joy.

To my family, Todd, Rory and Will, thank you for believing in me; for sacrificing so many weekends, evenings and vacations; and for fuelling me with coffee and snacks. Home, for me, is wherever you three are.

Photo Credits

Shutterstock

Anna Polukhina: 67 (top right); Anton_Ivanov: 41 (middle); Catalin Lazar: 46; Cheng Wei: 31 (bottom); cpaulfell: 9; EarnestTse: 2–3; elvistudio: 62; Felix Lipov: 51 (top); Gertan: 39; Global Pic's: 42; Greg da Silva: 50; HelloRF Zcool: 66; javarman: 11; Kiev.Victor: 24 (right); LALS STOCK: 38; mandritoiu: 8–31 (NYC banner); marchello74: 58; margaret tong: 10 (top); MasterPhoto: 43; Matyas Rehak: 70; Paul Stringer: 32–33 (world map); Peter Hermes Furian: 36 (bottom); Pra_Deep: 47 (top middle); rathshiki: 30 (top); Roman Yanushevsky: 35 (bottom left); Tatsuo Nakamura: 8; tenkl: 54; TierneyMJ: 17 (middle right).

Tyler Hicks / The New York Times: 26 (bottom left).

U.S. Department of Housing and Urban Development Office of Policy Development and Research: 21 (bottom right).

Wurts Bros. / Museum of the City of New York: X2010.7.1.5834: 15 (top right); X2010.7.2.26219: 18 (left).

zyxeos30 / iStock: 10 (bottom).

Index